POST-CAPITALIST SOCIETY

Books by Peter F. Drucker

MANAGEMENT
Managing for the Future
Managing the Non-Profit Organization
The Frontiers of Management
Innovation and Entrepreneurship
The Changing World of the Executive
Managing in Turbulent Times
Management: Tasks, Responsibilities, Practices
Technology, Management and Society
The Effective Executive
Managing for Results
The Practice of Management
Concept of the Corporation

ECONOMICS, POLITICS, SOCIETY
Post-Capitalist Society
The Ecological Vision
The New Realities
Toward the Next Economics
The Unseen Revolution
Men, Ideas and Politics
The Age of Discontinuity
Landmarks of Tomorrow
America's Next Twenty Years
The New Society
The Future of Industrial Man
The End of Economic Man

FICTION
The Temptation to Do Good
The Last of All Possible Worlds

AUTOBIOGRAPHY
Adventures of a Bystander

PETER F. DRUCKER

POST-CAPITALIST SOCIETY

HarperBusiness
A Division of HarperCollins*Publishers*

HarperCollins books may be purchased for educational, business, or sales promotional use. For information please write: Special Markets Department, HarperCollins Publishers, Inc., 10 East 53rd Street, New York, NY 10022.

FIRST EDITION

Designed by Alma Hochhauser Orenstein

Library of Congress Cataloging-in-Publication Data

Drucker, Peter Ferdinand
    Post-capitalist society / by Peter F. Drucker.—1st ed.
      p.   cm.
    Includes bibliographical references and index.
    ISBN 0-88730-620-9
    1. Economic history—1990–   2. Capitalism.   3. World
politics—1989–   4. Information society.   I. Title.
HC59.15.D78   1993
330.9′049—dc20   92-54323

93 94 95 96 97 PS/RRD 10 9 8 7 6 5 4 3 2 1

Contents

Introduction:
The Transformation

E very few hundred years in Western history there occurs a sharp transformation. We cross what in an earlier book* I called a "divide." Within a few short decades, society rearranges itself—its worldview; its basic values; its social and political structure; its arts; its key institutions. Fifty years later, there is a new world. And the people born then cannot even imagine the world in which their grandparents lived and into which their own parents were born.

We are currently living through just such a transformation. It is creating the post-capitalist society, which is the subject of this book.

One such transformation occurred in the thirteenth century, when the European world, almost overnight, became centered in the new city—with the emergence of city guilds as the new dominant social groups and with the revival of long-distance trade; with the Gothic, that eminently urban, practically bourgeois, new

* *The New Realities* (1989).

architecture; with the new painting of the Sienese; with the shift to Aristotle as the fountainhead of wisdom; with urban universities replacing as the centers of culture the monasteries in their rural isolation; with the new urban Orders, the Dominicans and Franciscans, emerging as the carriers of religion, of learning, of spirituality; and within a few decades, with the shift from Latin to the vernacular and with Dante's creation of European literature.

Two hundred years later, the next transformation took place in the sixty years between Johannes Gutenberg's invention in 1455 of printing with movable type and Martin Luther's Protestant Reformation in 1517. These were the decades of the blossoming of the Renaissance, peaking between 1470 and 1500 in Florence and Venice; of the rediscovery of antiquity; of the European discovery of America; of the Spanish Infantry, the first standing army since the Roman legions; of the rediscovery of anatomy and with it of scientific inquiry; and of the general adoption of Arabic numerals in the West. And again, no one living in 1520 could have imagined the world in which their grandparents had lived and into which their parents had been born.

The next transformation began in 1776—the year of the American Revolution, of James Watt's perfected steam engine, and of Adam Smith's *Wealth of Nations*. It came to a conclusion almost forty years later, at Waterloo—forty years during which all the modern "isms" were born. Capitalism, Communism, and the Industrial Revolution emerged during these decades. These years saw the creation—in 1809—of the modern university (Berlin), and also of universal schooling. These four decades brought the emancipation of the Jews—and by 1815, the Rothschilds had become the great power, overshadowing kings and princes. These forty years produced, in effect, a new European civilization. Again, no one living in 1820 could imagine the world in which their grandparents had lived and into which their parents had been born.

Our period, two hundred years later, is such a period of transformation. This time it is not, however, confined to Western society and Western history. Indeed, it is one of the fundamental changes that there no longer is a "Western" history or, in fact, a "Western" civilization. There is only world history and world civilization—but both are "Westernized." It is moot whether this present transformation began with the emergence of the first non-Western country, Japan, as a great economic power—that is, around 1960—or with the computer—that is, with information becoming central. My own candidate would be the American G.I. Bill of Rights after World War II, which gave every returning American soldier the money to attend a university—something that would have made absolutely no sense only thirty years earlier, at the end of World War I. The G.I. Bill of Rights—and the enthusiastic response to it on the part of America's veterans—signaled the shift to the knowledge society. Future historians may well consider it the most important event of the twentieth century.

We are clearly still in the middle of this transformation; indeed, if history is any guide, it will not be completed until 2010 or 2020. But already it has changed the political, economic, social, and moral landscape of the world. No one born in 1990 could possibly imagine the world in which one's grandparents (i.e., my generation) had grown up, or the world in which one's own parents had been born.

The first successful attempt to understand the transformation that turned the Middle Ages and the Renaissance into the modern world, the transformation that began in 1455, was not even attempted until fifty years later: with the *Commentaries* of Copernicus, written between 1510 and 1514; with Machiavelli's *The Prince*, written in 1513; with Michelangelo's synthesis and transcendence of all Renaissance art in the ceiling of the Sistine Chapel, painted between 1508 and 1512; and with the re-establishment of the Catholic Church at the Tridentine Council in the 1540s.

The next transformation—the one that occurred some two hundred years ago and was ushered in by the American Revolution—was first understood and analyzed sixty years afterward, in the two volumes of Alexis de Tocqueville's *Democracy in America*, published respectively in 1835 and 1840.

We are far enough advanced into the new post-capitalist society to review and revise the social, economic, and political history of the Age of Capitalism and of the nation-state. This book will therefore take new looks at the period we are leaving behind . . . and some of the things it sees from its new vantage point may come as distinct surprises (they did to me).

To foresee what the post-capitalist world itself will look like is, however, risky still. What new questions will arise and where the big new issues will lie, we can, I believe, already discover with some degree of probability. In many areas we can also describe what will not work. "Answers" to most questions are still largely hidden in the womb of the future. The one thing we can be sure of is that the world that will emerge from the present rearrangement of values, beliefs, social and economic structures, of political concepts and systems, indeed, of worldviews, will be different from anything anyone today imagines. In some areas—and especially in society and its structure—basic shifts have already happened. That the new society will be both a non-socialist and a post-capitalist society is practically certain. And it is certain also that its primary resource will be knowledge. This also means that it will have to be a society of organizations. Certain it is that in politics we have already shifted from the four hundred years of the sovereign nation-state to a pluralism in which the nation-state will be one rather than the only unit of political integration. It will be one component—though still a key component—in what I call the "post-capitalist polity," a system in which transnational, regional, nation-state, and local, even tribal, structures compete and co-exist.

These things have already happened. They can therefore be described. To do so is the purpose of this book.

POST-CAPITALIST SOCIETY
AND POST-CAPITALIST POLITY

Only a few short decades ago, everybody "knew" that a post-capitalist society would surely be a Marxist one. Now we all know that a Marxist society is the one thing the next society is not going to be. But most of us also know—or at least sense—that developed countries are moving out of anything that could be called "capitalism." The market will surely remain the effective integrator of *economic* activity. But as a society, the developed countries have also already moved into post-capitalism. It is fast becoming a society of new "classes," with a new central resource at its core.

Capitalist society was dominated by two social classes: the capitalists, who owned and controlled the means of production, and the workers—Karl Marx's "proletarians," alienated, exploited, dependent. The proletarians first became the "affluent" middle class as a result of the "Productivity Revolution"—the revolution that began at the very time of Marx's death in 1883, and reached its climax in every developed country shortly after World War II. Around 1950, the industrial worker—no longer a "proletarian" but still "labor"—seemed to dominate politics and society in every developed country. But then, with the onset of the "Management Revolution," the blue-collar workers in manufacturing industry rapidly began to decline both in numbers and, even more noticeably, in power and status. By the year 2000 there will be no developed country where traditional workers making and moving goods account for more than one sixth or one eighth of the work force.

The capitalist probably reached his peak even earlier—by the turn of the century, and surely no later than World War I. Since then, no one has matched in power and visibility the likes of Morgan, Rockefeller, Carnegie, or Ford in the United States; Siemens, Thyssen, Rathenau, Krupp in Germany; Mond, Cunard, Lever, Vickers, Armstrong in Great Britain; de Wendel and Schneider in France; or of the families that owned the great *zaibatsu* of Japan: Mitsubishi, Mitsui, and Sumitomo. By World War II they had all been replaced by "professional managers"*— the first result of the Management Revolution. There are still a great many rich people around, of course, and they are still prominent in newspaper society pages. But they have become

* The best account of this shift, though it is limited to manufacturing in the United States, is Alfred D. Chandler's *The Visible Hand* (Cambridge, Mass.: Harvard University Press, 1977).

"celebrities"; economically, they have almost ceased to matter. Even on the business page all the attention is being paid to "hired hands," that is, to managers. And such talk of money as there is is about the "excessive salaries" and bonuses of these hired hands, who themselves own little or nothing.

Instead of the old-line capitalist, in developed countries pension funds increasingly control the supply and allocation of money. In the United States, these funds in 1992 owned half of the share capital of the country's large businesses and held almost as much of these companies' fixed debts. The beneficiary owners of the pension funds are, of course, the country's employees. If Socialism is defined, as Marx defined it, as ownership of the means of production by the employees, then the United States has become the most "socialist" country around—while still remaining the most "capitalist" one as well. Pension funds are run by a new breed of capitalists: the faceless, anonymous, salaried employees, the pension funds' investment analysts and portfolio managers.

But equally important: the real, controlling resource and the absolutely decisive "factor of production" is now neither capital nor land nor labor. It is knowledge. Instead of capitalists and proletarians, the classes of the post-capitalist society are knowledge workers and service workers.

THE SHIFT TO THE KNOWLEDGE SOCIETY

The move to the post-capitalist society began shortly after World War II. I first wrote of the "employee society" even before 1950.* Ten years later, around 1960, I coined the terms "knowledge work" and "knowledge worker." And my *The Age of Discontinuity* (1969) first talked of the "society of organizations." *Post-Capitalist Society* is thus based on work done over forty years. Most of its policy and action recommendations have been successfully tested.

* See for example, *The New Society* (1949).

6

Only with the collapse of Marxism as an ideology and of Communism as a system,* however, did it become completely clear that we have already moved into a new and different society. Only then did a book like this become possible: a book that is not prediction but description, a book that is not *futuristic but a call to action here and now.*

The bankruptcy—moral, political, economic—of Marxism and the collapse of the Communist regimes were not "The End of History" (as a widely publicized 1989 article proclaimed).† Even the staunchest believers in the free market surely hesitate to hail its triumph as the Second Coming. But the events of 1989 and 1990 were more than just the end of an era; they signified the end of *one kind of history.* The collapse of Marxism and of Communism brought to a close two hundred and fifty years that were dominated by a secular religion—I have called it *the belief in salvation by society.* The first prophet of this secular religion was Jean-Jacques Rousseau (1712–1778). The Marxist Utopia was its ultimate distillation—and its apotheosis.

The same forces which destroyed Marxism as an ideology and Communism as a social system are, however, also making Capitalism obsolescent. For two hundred and fifty years, from the second half of the eighteenth century on, Capitalism was the dominant social reality. For the last hundred years, Marxism was the dominant social ideology. Both are rapidly being superseded by a new and very different society.

The new society—and it is already here—is a post-capitalist society. This new society surely, to say it again, will use the free market as the one proven mechanism of economic integration. It will not be an "anti-capitalist society." It will not even be a "non-capitalist society"; the institutions of Capitalism will survive, although some, such as banks, may play quite different roles. But

* Both anticipated in *The New Realities*, written in 1986–7, several years ahead of the actual events.
† Francis Fukuyama's "The End of History," *The National Interest* (Summer 1989).

the center of gravity in the post-capitalist society—its structure, its social and economic dynamics, its social classes, and its social problems—is different from the one that dominated the last two hundred and fifty years and defined the issues around which political parties, social groups, social value systems, and personal and political commitments crystallized.

The basic economic resource—"the means of production," to use the economist's term—is no longer capital, nor natural resources (the economist's "land"), nor "labor." *It is and will be knowledge*. The central wealth-creating activities will be neither the allocation of capital to productive uses, nor "labor"—the two poles of nineteenth- and twentieth-century economic theory, whether classical, Marxist, Keynesian, or neo-classical. Value is now created by "productivity" and "innovation," both applications of knowledge to work. The leading social groups of the knowledge society will be "knowledge workers"— knowledge executives who know how to allocate knowledge to productive use, just as the capitalists knew how to allocate capital to productive use; knowledge professionals; knowledge employees. Practically all these knowledge people will be employed in organizations. Yet, unlike the employees under Capitalism, they will own both the "means of production" and the "tools of production"—the former through their pension funds, which are rapidly emerging in all developed countries as the only real owners; the latter because knowledge workers own their knowledge and can take it with them wherever they go. The *economic* challenge of the post-capitalist society will therefore be the productivity of knowledge work and the knowledge worker.

The *social* challenge of the post-capitalist society will, however, be the dignity of the second class in post-capitalist society: the service workers. Service workers, as a rule, lack the necessary education to be knowledge workers. And in every country, even the most highly advanced one, they will constitute a majority.

The post-capitalist society will be divided by a new dichotomy of values and of aesthetic perceptions. It will not be the "Two Cultures"—literary and scientific—of which the English novelist, scientist, and government administrator C. P. Snow wrote in his

The Two Cultures and the Scientific Revolution (1959), though that split is real enough. The dichotomy will be between "intellectuals" and "managers," the former concerned with words and ideas, the latter with people and work. To transcend this dichotomy in a new synthesis will be a central philosophical and educational challenge for the post-capitalist society.

OUTFLANKING THE NATION-STATE

The late 1980s and early 1990s also marked the end of another era, another "kind of history." If the fall of the Berlin Wall in 1989 was the climactic event that symbolized the fall of Marxism and Communism, the transnational coalition against Iraq's invasion of Kuwait in 1990 was the climactic event that marked the end of four hundred years of history in which the sovereign nation-state was the main, and often the only, actor on the political stage.

Future historians will surely rank February 1991 among the "big dates." There is no precedent for such transnational action. At no earlier occasion did nations—without a single dissenter of consequence (and almost without dissent altogether)—set the common interest of the world community in putting down terrorism ahead of their own national sentiments, and, in many cases, ahead even of their own national interest. There is no precedent for the all but universal realization that terrorism is not a matter of "politics" to be left to individual national governments, but requires transnational action.

> It is widely believed, especially among so-called liberals in the United States, that the 1991 war against Iraq was mounted to protect the West's oil supply. Nothing could be further from the truth. Iraqi control of the oil wells of Kuwait—and those of Saudi Arabia as well—would have been very much in the West's *economic* interest; it would have meant much cheaper oil. For while Kuwait and Saudi Arabia have practically no native population and therefore no urgent need for immediate petroleum income, Iraq is heavily overpopulated, and, except for petroleum, almost totally

without natural resources. It therefore needs to sell as much oil as it possibly can, whereas Kuwait and Saudi Arabia are primarily interested in keeping oil prices high, which means keeping production low.

This, by the way, explains why the United States heavily supported Saddam Hussein's regime in Iraq, even before the Iran-Iraq War, and why it continued to do so until the very moment when Saddam attacked Kuwait and thus indulged in an overt terrorist act. It also explains, I suspect, why Saddam miscalculated; he must have been convinced that the United States would let him get away with flagrant aggression in order to ensure low petroleum prices. And everyone I spoke to in one major petroleum company was sure when Iraq invaded Kuwait that the U.S. government would not do anything but make a few disapproving noises.

In the four hundred years since the French lawyer-politician Jean Bodin (1530–1596) invented it (in his *Six Livres de la République*, published in 1576), the nation-state became the sole organ of political power, both internally and externally. And during the past two hundred years, since the French Revolution, it has also become the carrier of the secular religion, the belief in salvation by society. In fact, totalitarianism—Communist as well as Nazi— was the ultimate distillation and apotheosis of the doctrine of the sovereign nation-state as the one and only organ of power.

Political theory and constitutional law still know only the sovereign state. And in the last hundred years this state has steadily become more powerful and more dominant, mutating into a "megastate." It is the one political structure we so far understand, are familiar with, and know how to build out of prefabricated and standardized parts: an executive, a legislature, courts, a diplomatic service, national armies, and so on. Every one of the nearly 200 new countries that have been carved out of the former colonial empires since the end of World War II has been set up as a sovereign nation-state. And this is what every one of the various parts of the last of the colonial empires, the Soviet Empire, aspires to become.

And yet for forty years, since the end of World War II, the sovereign nation-state has steadily been losing its position as the *sole* organ of power. Internally, developed countries are fast becoming pluralist societies of organizations. Externally, some governmental functions are becoming transnational, others regional, in the European Community, for example; and others are being tribalized.

The nation-state is not going to wither away. It may remain the most powerful political organ around for a long time to come, but it will no longer be the indispensable one. Increasingly, it will share power with other organs, other institutions, other policymakers. What is to remain the domain of the nation-state? What is to be carried out within the state by autonomous institutions? How do we define "supranational" and "transnational"? What should remain "separate and local"?

These questions will be central political issues for decades to come. In its specifics, the outcome is quite unpredictable. But the political order will look different from the political order of the last four centuries, in which the players differed in size, wealth, constitutional arrangements, and political creed, yet were uniform as nation-states—each sovereign within its territory and each defined by its territory. We are moving—we have indeed already moved—into *post-capitalist polity*.

The last of what might be called the "pre-modern" philosophers, Gottfried Leibniz (1646–1716), spent much of his life in a futile attempt to restore the unity of Christendom. His motivation was not the fear of religious wars between Catholics and Protestants or between different Protestant sects; that danger had already passed when Leibniz was born. He feared that without a common belief in a supernatural God, secular religions would emerge. And a secular religion, he was convinced, would, almost by definition, have to be a tyranny and suppress the freedom of the person.

A century later, Jean-Jacques Rousseau confirmed Leibniz's fears. Rousseau asserted that *society* could and should control the individual human being. It could and should create a "New Adam." It could and should create universal human perfection. But it also could and should subordinate the individual to the

impersonal, super-personal *volonté générale* (the general will)—
what Marxists later came to call the "objective laws of history."
Since the French Revolution, salvation by society has gradually
evolved into the dominant creed—first in the West, then later
(since the start of World War II) worldwide. However much it
pretends to be "anti-religious," this is a religious faith. The means
are, of course, non-spiritual: banning liquor; killing all Jews;
psychoanalysis for everybody; abolition of private property. The
goal however, is religious: to establish the Kingdom of God on
Earth by creating the "New Man."

For more than a hundred years, the most powerful and the
most pervasive secular creed promising salvation through society
was Marxism. The religious promise of Marxism, far more than
its convoluted ideology and its increasingly unrealistic economics, constituted its tremendous appeal, especially to intellectuals. There were many reasons, for instance, for Eastern Jews to
accept an ideology that promised an end to discrimination and
persecution against them in Romania or the Russia of the tsars.
But the most powerful appeal for them was Marxism's promise of
an earthly paradise, that is, Marxism's appeal as a secular
religion.

Communism collapsed as an economic system. Instead of
creating wealth, it created misery. Instead of creating economic
equality, it created a *nomenklatura* of functionaries enjoying unprecedented economic privileges. But as a creed, Marxism collapsed because it did not succeed in creating the "New Man."
Instead, it brought out and strengthened all the worst in the
"Old Adam": corruption, greed, and lust for power; envy and
mutual distrust; petty tyranny and secretiveness; lying, stealing,
denunciation, and, above all, cynicism. Communism, the system,
had its heroes. But Marxism, the creed, did not have a single
saint.

The human being may well be beyond redemption. The
Latin poet may have been right: human nature always sneaks in
through the back door, no matter how many times the pitchfork
tosses it out the front. Maybe the cynics are right in asserting that
there is no virtue, no goodness, no selflessness, only self-interest

and hypocrisy (although there are enough witnesses to the contrary, as I remind myself in my darkest hours).

But surely the collapse of Marxism as a creed signifies the end of the belief in salvation by society. What will emerge next, we cannot know; we can only hope and pray. Perhaps nothing beyond stoic resignation? Perhaps a rebirth of traditional religion, addressing itself to the needs and challenges of the person in the knowledge society? The explosive growth of what I call "pastoral" Christian churches in America—Protestant, Catholic, non-denominational—might be a portent. But so might be the resurgence of fundamentalist Islam. For the young people in the Muslim world who now so fervently embrace Islamic fundamentalism would, forty years ago, have been equally fervent Marxists. Or will there be new religions?*

Still, redemption, self-renewal, spiritual growth, goodness, and virtue—the "New Man," to use the traditional term—are likely to be seen again as existential rather than social goals or political prescriptions. The end of the belief in salvation by society surely marks an inward turning. It makes possible renewed emphasis on the individual, the person. It may even lead—at least we can so hope—to a return to individual responsibility.

THE THIRD WORLD

This book focuses on the developed countries: on Europe, the United States, and Canada, on Japan and the newly developed countries on the mainland of Asia, rather than on the developing countries of the "Third World."

This is not because I consider the less developed nations unimportant or even less important. That would be folly. Two

* What is unlikely is easier to forecast than what is likely. We will not, for example, see the rejection of material values and of technology, that "return to the Middle Ages" which a Japanese writer, Taichi Sakaya, predicted in a best-seller of the mid-1980s (published in English in 1991 by Kodansha International under the title *The Knowledge-Value Revolution*). The worldwide spread of information and of technology is certain to make this impossible.

thirds of the world's population live, after all, in the Third World; and by the time the present period of transition comes to an end (around 2010 or 2020), the Third World will house three quarters. But I also consider it highly probable that within the next decade or two there will be new and startling "economic miracles," in which poor, backward Third World countries transform themselves, virtually overnight, into fast-growth economic powers. It is even possible that there will be far more such transformations than there have been in the last forty years, since we first began to talk about "economic development."

All the elements for rapid economic growth are present in the coastal, urbanized areas of Mainland China—from Tianjin (Tientsin) in the north to Canton in the south. They have a huge domestic market; a highly educated population with tremendous respect for learning; an ancient entrepreneurial tradition; and close ties to the "Overseas Chinese" in Singapore, Hong Kong, and Taiwan, with access to their capital, their trading networks, and their knowledgeable people. All this might be released in an explosion of entrepreneurial growth if Beijing's political and economic tyranny could be peacefully removed. Similarly, Latin America's larger countries offer an adequate domestic market. Mexico may already be in the "takeoff" stage. And Brazil might surprise everybody by the speed of its turnaround once it musters the political courage to follow Mexico's recent example and abandon the failed, indeed suicidal, policies into which it plunged after 1970. No one can possibly foretell what surprises the former Communist countries of Eastern Europe might produce.

But the developed countries also have a tremendous stake in the Third World. Unless there is rapid development there—both economic and social—the developed countries will be inundated by a human flood of Third World immigrants far beyond their economic, social, or cultural capacity to absorb.

But the forces that are creating post-capitalist society and post-capitalist polity originate in the developed world. They are the product and result of its development. Answers to the challenges of post-capitalist society and post-capitalist polity will not be found in the Third World. If anything has been totally disproven, it is the promises of the Third World leaders of the fifties and sixties—Nehru in India, Mao in China, Castro in Cuba, Tito in Yugoslavia, the apostles of *"Négritude"* in Africa, or Neo-Marxists like Che Guevara. They promised that the Third World would find new and different answers, and would, in fact, create a new order. The Third World has not delivered on these promises made in its name. The challenges, the opportunities, the problems of post-capitalist society and post-capitalist polity can only be dealt with where they originated. And that is in the developed world.

SOCIETY, POLITY, KNOWLEDGE

This book covers a wide range. It deals with post-capitalist society; with post-capitalist polity; and with new challenges to knowledge itself. Yet it leaves out much more than it attempts to cover. It is not a history of the future. Rather, it is *a look at the present*.

The areas of discussion—Society, Polity, Knowledge—are not arrayed in order of importance. That would have put first the short discussion of the educated person which concludes this work. The three areas are arrayed *in order of predictability*. With respect to the post-capitalist *society*, we know what has happened and why; we know what is going to happen and why—at least in outline—and a good deal is already happening. With respect to the post-capitalist *polity*, we have only programs so far. How the needed changes will be brought about is still conjecture. But we know what has happened and why; we can specify what needs to happen and why. With respect to the *knowledge* challenges, however, we can only ask questions—and hope that they are the right questions.

I am often asked whether I am an optimist or a pessimist. For any survivor of this century to be an optimist would be fatuous. We surely are nowhere near the end of the turbulences, the transformations, the sudden upsets, which have made this century one of the meanest, cruelest, bloodiest in human history. Anyone who deludes him- or herself that we are anywhere near the "end of history" is in for unpleasant surprises—the kind of surprises that afflicted America's President George Bush when he first bet on the survival of the Soviet Empire under Michail Gorbachev, and then on the success of Boris Yeltsin's "Commonwealth of ex-Russian Nations."

Nothing "post" is permanent or even long-lived. Ours is a transition period. What the future society will look like, let alone whether it will indeed be the "knowledge society" some of us dare hope for, depends on how the developed countries respond to the challenges of this transition period, the post-capitalist period— their intellectual leaders, their business leaders, their political leaders, but above all each of us in our own work and life. Yet surely this is a time to *make the future*—precisely because everything is in flux. This is a time for action.

PART ONE

SOCIETY

1

From Capitalism to Knowledge Society

WITHIN ONE HUNDRED FIFTY YEARS, from 1750 to 1900, capitalism and technology conquered the globe and created a world civilization. Neither capitalism nor technical innovations were new; both had been common, recurrent phenomena throughout the ages, in West and East alike. What was brand new was their speed of diffusion and their global reach across cultures, classes, and geography. And it was this speed and scope that converted capitalism into "Capitalism" and into a "system," and technical advances into the "Industrial Revolution."

This transformation was driven by a radical change in the meaning of knowledge. In both West and East, knowledge had always been seen as applying to *being*. Then, almost overnight, it came to be applied to *doing*. It became a resource and a utility. Knowledge had always been a private good. Almost overnight it became a public good.

For a hundred years—during the first phase—knowledge was applied to tools, processes, products. This created the Industrial Revolution. But it also created what Karl Marx (1818–1883) called "alienation," new classes and class war, and with them

Communism. In its second phase, beginning around 1880 and culminating around the end of World War II, knowledge in its new meaning came to be applied to work. This ushered in the *Productivity Revolution*, which in seventy-five years converted the proletarian into a middle-class bourgeois with near-upper-class income. The Productivity Revolution thus defeated class war and Communism.

The last phase began after World War II. Today, knowledge is being applied to *knowledge* itself. This is the *Management Revolution*. Knowledge is now fast becoming the sole factor of production, sidelining both capital and labor. It may be premature (and certainly would be presumptuous) to call ours a "knowledge society"; so far, we have only a knowledge economy. But our society is surely "post-capitalist."

Capitalism, in one form or another, has occurred and reoccurred many times throughout the ages, in the East as well as in the West. And there have been numerous earlier periods of rapid technical invention and innovation—again in the East as well as the West—many of them producing technical changes fully as radical as any in the late eighteenth or early nineteenth centuries.* What is unprecedented and unique about the developments of the last two hundred fifty years is their speed and scope. Instead of being one element in society, as all earlier capitalism had been, Capitalism—with a capital C—became so-

---

* The best discussion of capitalism as a recurrent and fairly frequent phenomenon can be found in two works by the great French economic historian Fernand Braudel: *The Mediterranean* (2 vols., first published in France in 1949; English translation, New York: Harper & Row, 1972); and *Civilization and Capitalism* (3 vols., first published in France in 1979; English translation, New York: Harper & Row, 1981). The best discussions of earlier "industrial revolutions" are *Medieval Technology and Social Change*, by Lynn White, Jr. (Oxford University Press, 1962); *The Medieval Machine: The Industrial Revolution of the Middle Ages*, by Jean Gimpel (first published in France in 1975; English translation, New York: Holt, Rinehart & Winston, 1976); and the monumental *Science and Civilization in China* by the British biochemist, orientalist, and historian Joseph Needham (Cambridge University Press), publication of which began in 1954 with half of the planned twenty-five parts yet to appear. What Needham has published so far has already completely changed our knowledge of early technology. For earlier "industrial revolutions," see also my *Technology, Management and Society* (1973), especially Chapters 3, 7, and 11.

---

ciety. Instead of being confined, as always before, to a narrow locality, Capitalism—again with a capital C—took over all of Western and Northern Europe in a mere one hundred years, from 1750 to 1850. Then, within another fifty years, it took over the entire inhabited world.

All earlier capitalism had been confined to small, narrow groups in society. Nobles, landowners, the military, peasants, professionals, craftsmen, even laborers, were almost untouched by it. Capitalism with a capital C soon permeated and transformed all groups in society wherever it spread.

From earliest times in the Old World, new tools, new processes, new materials, new crops, new techniques—what we now call "technology"—diffused swiftly.

Few modern inventions, for instance, spread as fast as a thirteenth-century one: eyeglasses. Derived from the optical experiments of an English Franciscan friar, Roger Bacon (d. 1292 or 1294), around 1270, reading glasses for the elderly were in use at the papal court of Avignon by 1290, at the Sultan's court in Cairo by 1300, and at the court of the Mongol emperor of China no later than 1310. Only the sewing machine and the telephone, fastest-spreading of all nineteenth-century inventions, moved as swiftly.

But earlier technological change almost without exception remained confined to one craft or one application. It took another two hundred years—until the early 1500s—before Bacon's invention had its second application: eyeglasses to correct nearsightedness. The potter's wheel was in full use in the Mediterranean by 1500 B.C.; pots for cooking, and for storing water and food, were available in every household. Yet the principle underlying the potter's wheel was not applied until A.D. 1000 to women's work: spinning.

Similarly, the redesign of the windmill around the year 800, which converted it from the toy it had been in antiquity into a true machine (and a fully "automated" one at that), was not applied to ships for more than three hundred years, after 1100. Until then, ships used oars; if wind was used at all to propel them, it was as an auxiliary power, and then only if it blew in the right direction. The sail that drives a ship works exactly the same way as the sail that drives the windmill, and the need for a sail that would enable a ship to sail cross-wind and against the wind had been known for a long time. The windmill was redesigned in Northern France or in the Low Countries, both regions thoroughly familiar with ships and navigation. Yet it did not occur to anyone for several hundred years to apply something invented to pump water and to grind corn—for use on land—to use offshore.

The inventions of the Industrial Revolution, however, were immediately applied across the board, and across all conceivable crafts and industries. They were immediately seen as *technology*.

James Watt's (1736–1819) redesign of the steam engine between 1765 and 1776 made it into a cost-effective provider of power. Watt himself throughout his own productive life focused on one use only: to pump water out of a mine—the use for which the steam engine had first been designed by Thomas Newcomen in the early years of the eighteenth century. But one of England's leading ironmasters immediately saw that the redesigned steam engine could also be used to blow air into a blast furnace and bid for the second engine Watt had built. And Watt's partner, Matthew Boulton (1728–1809), right away promoted the steam engine as a provider of power for all kinds of industrial processes, especially the largest of all manufacturing industries, textiles. Thirty-five years later an American, Robert Fulton (1765–1815), floated the first steamship on New York's Hudson River. Another twenty years later the steam engine was put on wheels and the locomotive was born. And by 1840—or at the very latest 1850—the steam engine had transformed every single manufacturing process from glass-making to printing. It had transformed long-distance transportation on land and sea, and it was beginning to transform farming. By then, it had penetrated almost the entire world—Tibet, Nepal, and the interior of tropical Africa being the sole exceptions.

The nineteenth century believed—and most people still believe—that the Industrial Revolution was the first time a change in the "mode of production" (to use Karl Marx's term) changed social structure and created new classes, the capitalist and the proletarian. But this belief, too, is invalid. Between 700 and 1100 A.D., two brand-new classes were created in Europe by technological change: those of the feudal knight and the urban craftsman. The knight was created by the invention of the stirrup—an invention that arose in Central Asia around the year 700; the craftsman by the redesign of water wheel and windmill into true machines which, for the first time, used inanimate forces (water and wind) as motive power rather than human muscle.

The stirrup made it possible to fight on horseback; without it, a rider wielding lance, sword, or heavy bow would immediately have been thrown off his horse by the force of Newton's Second Law: "To every action there is an equal and opposite reaction." For several hundred years, the knight remained an invincible "fighting machine." But this machine had to be supported by a "military-agricultural complex"—something quite new in history. Germans until this century called it a *Rittergut*, a knight's estate, endowed with legal status and economic and political privileges, and containing at least fifty peasant families or some two hundred people to produce the food needed to support the fighting machine: the knight, his squire, his three horses, and his twelve to fifteen grooms. The stirrup, in other words, created feudalism.

The craftsman of antiquity had been a slave. The craftsman of the first "machine age," the craftsman of Europe's Middle Ages, became the urban ruling class, the "burgher," who then created Europe's unique city, and both the Gothic and the Renaissance styles that followed.

The technical innovations—stirrup, water wheel, and windmill—traveled throughout the entire Old World, and fast. But the classes of the earlier industrial revolution remained European phenomena on the whole. Only in Japan, around 1100 A.D., did proud and independent craftsmen evolve, who enjoyed high esteem and, until 1600, considerable power. But while the Japanese adopted the stirrup for riding, they continued to fight on foot. The rulers in rural Japan were the commanders of foot soldiers—the *daimyo*. They levied taxes on the peasantry but had no feudal estates. In China, in India, in the world of Islam, the new technologies had no social impact whatever. Craftsmen in China remained serfs without social status. The military did not become landowners but remained, as in Europe's antiquity, professional mercenaries. Even in Europe, the social changes generated by this early industrial revolution took almost four hundred years to take full effect.

By contrast, the social transformation of society brought about by Capitalism and Industrial Revolution took less than a hundred years to become fully effective in Western Europe. In 1750, capitalists and proletarians were still marginal groups; in fact, proletarians in the nineteenth-century meaning of the term, that is, factory workers, hardly existed at all. By 1850, capitalists and proletarians were the dynamic classes of Western Europe, and were on the offensive. They rapidly became the dominant classes wherever capitalism and modern technology penetrated. In Japan, the transformation took less than thirty years, from the Meiji Restoration in 1867 to the war with China in 1894. It took not much longer in Shanghai and Hong Kong, Calcutta and Bombay, or in the tsars' Russia.

Capitalism and the Industrial Revolution—because of their speed and their scope—created a world civilization.*

THE NEW MEANING OF KNOWLEDGE

Unlike those "terrible simplifiers," the nineteenth-century ideologues such as Hegel and Marx, we now know that major historical events rarely have just one cause and just one explanation. They typically result from the convergence of a good many separate and independent developments.

One example of how history works is the genesis of the computer. Its earliest root is the binary system, the realization of a seventeenth-century mathematician-philosopher, the German

---

* The best history of this development is *Prometheus Unbound*, by the Harvard historian David S. Landes (Cambridge University Press, 1969).

Gottfried Leibniz, that all numbers can be represented by just two: 0 and 1. The second root is the discovery of a nineteenth-century English inventor, Charles Babbage (1792–1871), that toothed wheels, that is, mechanics, could represent the entire decimal system and do all four elementary arithmetic functions: addition, subtraction, multiplication, and division—a genuine "computing machine." Then in the early years of this century, two English logicians, Alfred North Whitehead and Bertrand Russell, in their *Principia Mathematica* showed that any concept, if presented in rigorously logical form, can be expressed mathematically. From this discovery an Austro-American, Otto Neurath, working as statistician for the U.S. War Production Board of World War I, derived the idea, then brand new and heretical, that all information from any area is exactly the same when quantified, and can be treated and presented the same way (the idea, by the way, that also underlies modern statistics). A little earlier, just before World War I, an American, Lee De Forest, had invented the audion tube to convert electronic impulses into sound waves, thus making possible the broadcasting of speech and music. Twenty years later it occurred to engineers working at a medium-sized punch-card manufacturer, called IBM, that the audion tube could be used to switch electronically from 0 to 1 and back again.

If any of these elements had been missing, there would have been no computer. No one can say which of these was the essential element. With all of them in place, however, the computer became virtually inevitable. It was then pure accident that it became an American development—the accident of World War II, which made the American military willing to spend enormous sums on developing (quite unsuccessfully until well after World War II) machines to calculate at high speed the position of fast-moving aircraft overhead and of fast-moving enemy ships. Otherwise the computer would probably have become a British development. Indeed, an English company, the food producer and restaurant owner J. Lyons & Co., actually developed the first computer for commercial purposes that really worked, the "Leo," in the 1940s. Lyons just couldn't raise the money to compete with the Pentagon, and had to abandon its successful (and much cheaper) machine.

Many separate developments—most of them probably quite unconnected with each other—went into turning capitalism into Capitalism and technical advance into the Industrial Revolution. The best-known theory—that Capitalism was the child of the "Protestant Ethic"—was expounded in the opening years of this century by the German sociologist Max Weber (1864–1920). It has now been largely discredited; there just is not enough evidence for it. There is only a little more evidence to support Karl Marx's earlier thesis that the steam engine, the new prime mover, required such enormous capital investment that craftsmen could no longer finance their "means of production" and had to cede control to the capitalist.

There is one critical element, however, without which well-known phenomena—capitalism and technical advance—could not possibly have turned into a social and worldwide pandemic. That is the radical change in the *meaning of knowledge* that occurred in Europe around the year 1700, or shortly thereafter.*

There are as many theories as to what we can know and how we know it as there have been metaphysicians, from Plato in 400 B.C. to Ludwig Wittgenstein (1889–1951) and Karl Popper (b. 1902) in our own day. But since Plato's time there have only been two theories in the West—and since around the same time, two theories in the East—regarding the meaning and function of knowledge. Plato's spokesman, the wise Socrates, holds that the sole function of knowledge is self-knowledge: the intellectual, moral, and spiritual growth of the person. His ablest opponent, the brilliant and learned Protagoras, holds however that the purpose of knowledge is to make the holder effective by enabling him to know what to say and how to say it. For Protagoras, knowledge meant logic, grammar, and rhetoric—later to become the *trivium*, the core of learning in the Middle Ages, and still very

---

* This change is explored in some depth in my 1961 essay, "The Technological Revolution; Notes on the Relationship of Technology, Science and Culture," reprinted in *Technology, Management and Society* (1972), and in my *The Ecological Vision* (New Brunswick, N.J.: Transaction Publishers, 1992).

much what we mean by a "liberal education" or what the Germans mean by "*Allgemeine Bildung*." In the East, there were pretty much the same two theories of knowledge. Knowledge for the Confucian meant knowing what to say and how to say it as the route to advancement and earthly success. Knowledge for the Taoist and the Zen monk meant self-knowledge, and the road to enlightenment and wisdom. But while the two sides thus sharply disagreed about what knowledge actually meant, they were in total agreement as to what it did not mean. It did not mean *ability to do*. It did not mean *utility*. Utility was not knowledge; it was *skill*—the Greek word is *technē*.

Unlike their Far Eastern contemporaries, the Chinese Confucians with their infinite contempt for anything but book learning, both Socrates and Protagoras respected *technē*.*

But even to Socrates and Protagoras, *technē*, however commendable, was not knowledge. It was confined to one specific application and had no general principles. What the shipmaster knew about navigating from Greece to Sicily could not be applied to anything else. Furthermore, the only way to learn a *technē* was through apprenticeship and experience. A *technē* could not be explained in words, whether spoken or written; it could only be demonstrated. As late as 1700, or even later, the English did not speak of "crafts." They spoke of "mysteries"—not just because the possessor of a craft skill was sworn to secrecy but also because a craft by definition was inaccessible to anyone who had not been apprenticed to a master and thus learned by example.

THE INDUSTRIAL REVOLUTION

But then, beginning after 1700—and within an incredibly short fifty years—technology was invented. The very word is a manifesto in that it combines "*technē*," that is, the mystery of a craft

* In fact, in the West contempt for skill was unknown until England's eighteenth-century "gentleman." This contempt which reached such heights in Victorian England was surely little but a futile last-ditch defense against the gentleman's being replaced as society's ruling group by capitalist and technologist.

skill, with "logy," organized, systematic, purposeful knowledge. The first engineering school, the French *Ecole des Ponts et Chaussées*, was founded in 1747, followed around 1770 by the first School of Agriculture and in 1776 by the first School of Mining, both in Germany. In 1794, the first technical university, the French *Ecole Polytechnique*, was founded, and with it, the profession of engineer. Shortly thereafter, between 1820 and 1850, medical education and medical practice were reorganized as a systematic technology.

In a parallel development, Great Britain between 1750 and 1800 shifted from patents as monopolies to enrich royal favorites to patents granted to encourage the application of knowledge to tools, products, and processes, and in order to reward inventors, provided they published their inventions. This not only triggered a century of feverish mechanical invention in Britain; it put an end to craft mystery and secretiveness.

The great document of this dramatic shift from skill to technology—one of the most important books in history—was the *Encyclopédie*, edited between 1751 and 1772 by Denis Diderot (1713–1784) and Jean d'Alembert (1717–1783). This famous work attempted to bring together in organized and systematic form the knowledge of all crafts, in such a way that the non-apprentice could learn to be a "technologist." It was by no means accidental that articles in the *Encyclopédie* that describe an individual craft, such as spinning or weaving, were not written by craftsmen. They were written by "information specialists": people trained as analysts, as mathematicians, as logicians—both Voltaire and Rousseau were contributors. The underlying thesis of the *Encyclopédie* was that effective results in the material universe—in tools, processes, and product—are produced by systematic analysis, and by the systematic, purposeful application of knowledge.

But the *Encyclopédie* also preached that principles which produced results in one craft would produce results in any other. That was anathema, however, to both the traditional man of knowledge and the traditional craftsman.

None of the technical schools of the eighteenth century

aimed at producing *new* knowledge; nor did the *Encyclopédie*. None even talked of the application of *science* to tools, processes, and products, that is, to technology. This idea had to wait for another hundred years, until 1830 or so, when a German chemist, Justus von Liebig (1803–1873), applied science to invent, first, artificial fertilizers, and then a way to preserve animal protein: meat extract. What the early technical schools and the *Encyclopédie* did do, however, was perhaps more important. They brought together, codified, and published the *technē*, the craft mystery, as it had been developed over millennia. They converted experience into knowledge, apprenticeship into textbook, secrecy into methodology, doing into applied knowledge. These are the essentials of what we have come to call the "Industrial Revolution"—the transformation by technology of society and civilization worldwide.

It was this change in the meaning of knowledge which then made modern Capitalism inevitable and dominant. Above all, the speed of technical change created demand for capital way beyond anything the craftsman could possibly supply. The new technology also required concentration of production, that is, the shift to the factory. Knowledge could not be applied in tens of thousands of small individual workshops and in the cottage industries of the rural village. It required concentration of production under one roof.

The new technology also required large-scale energy, whether water power or steam power, which could not be decentralized. But, though important, these energy needs were secondary. The central point was that production almost overnight moved from being craft-based to being technology-based. As a result, the capitalist moved almost overnight into the center of economy and society. Before, he had always been "supporting cast."

As late as 1750, large-scale enterprise was governmental rather than private. The earliest, and for many centuries the greatest, of all manufacturing enterprises in the Old World was the famous arsenal owned and run by the government of Venice. And the eighteenth-century "manufactories" such as the porcelain works of Meissen and Sèvres were still government-owned.

But by 1830, large-scale private capitalist enterprise dominated in the West. Another fifty years later, by the time Marx died in 1883, private capitalist enterprise had penetrated everywhere except to such remote corners of the world as Tibet or the Empty Quarter of Arabia.

There was resistance, of course, both to technology and to capitalism. There were riots—in England, for instance, or in German Silesia. But these were local, lasted a few weeks or at most a few months, and did not even slow down the speed and spread of Capitalism.

The machine and the factory system spread equally fast and equally without meeting much resistance, if any.

Adam Smith's *Wealth of Nations* appeared in the same year in which James Watt patented the perfected steam engine. Yet the *Wealth of Nations* pays practically no attention to machines, factories, or industrial production. The production it describes is still craft-based. Even forty years later, after the Napoleonic Wars, factories and machines were not yet seen as central by acute social observers. They play practically no role in the economics of David Ricardo (1772–1823). Neither factory workers nor bankers can be found in the novels of Jane Austen, England's most perceptive social critic at the turn of the nineteenth century. Her society (as has often been said) is thoroughly "bourgeois." But it is still totally pre-industrial, a society of squires and tenants, parsons and naval officers, lawyers, craftsmen, and shopkeepers. Only in faraway America did Alexander Hamilton see very early that machine-based manufacturing was fast becoming the central economic activity. But few even among his followers paid much attention to his 1791 *Report on Manufactures* until long after his death in 1804.

By the 1830s, however, Honoré de Balzac was turning out bestselling novel after bestselling novel depicting a capitalist France whose society was dominated by bankers and by the stock exchange. Another fifteen years later, the factory system and the machine are central in the mature works of Charles Dickens, and so are the new classes, the capitalists and the proletarians. In *Bleak House* (1852–53), the new society and its tensions form the subplot in the contrast between two able brothers, both sons of the squire's housekeeper. One becomes a great industrialist in the North, who plans to get himself elected to Parliament to fight the landowners and break their power. The other chooses to remain a loyal retainer of the broken, defeated, ineffectual (but pre-capitalist) "gentleman." And Dickens's *Hard Times* (1854) is the first and by far the most powerful industrial novel, the story of a bitter strike in a cotton mill and of class war at its starkest.

The unheard-of speed with which society was transformed created the social tensions and conflicts of the new order. We now know that there is no truth in the all but universal belief that factory workers in the early nineteenth century were worse off and were treated more harshly than they had been as landless laborers in the pre-industrial countryside. They were badly off, no doubt, and harshly treated. But they flocked to the factory precisely because they were still better off there than they were at the bottom of a static, tyrannical, and starving rural society. They still experienced a much better "quality of life." "England's green and pleasant land" which William Blake (1757–1827) in his famous poem *The New Jerusalem* hoped to liberate from the new "Satanic Mills," was in reality one vast rural slum.*

While industrialization, from the beginning, meant material improvement rather than Marx's famous "immiseration," the speed of change was so breathtaking as to be deeply traumatic. The new class, the "proletarians," became "alienated," to use the term Marx coined. Their alienation, he predicted, would make inevitable their exploitation. For they were becoming totally dependent for their livelihood on access to the "means of production," which were owned and controlled by the capitalist. This in turn—so Marx predicted—would increasingly concentrate own-

---

* We should have known this all along, by the way. In the factory town, infant mortality immediately went down and life expectancies immediately went up, thus triggering the enormous population growth of industrializing Europe. But we also have the example of the Third World countries since World War II. Brazilians and Peruvians stream into the *favelas* and *barrios* of Rio de Janeiro and Lima. However hard, life there is better than in the impoverished *Noreste* of Brazil or on Peru's *Altiplano*. Indians today say: "The poorest beggar in Bombay still eats better than the farm hand in the village."

ership in fewer and bigger hands, and increasingly impoverish a powerless proletariat—until the day at which the system would collapse under its own weight, the few remaining capitalists overthrown by proletarians who "had nothing to lose but their chains."

We know now that Marx was a false prophet—the very opposite of what he predicted has in fact happened. But this is hindsight. Most of his contemporaries shared his view of capitalism, even if they did not necessarily share his prediction of the outcome. Even anti-Marxists accepted Marx's analysis of the "inherent contradictions of capitalism." Some were confident that the military would keep the proletarian rabble in check, as was apparently the greatest of nineteenth-century capitalists, the American banker J. P. Morgan (1837–1913). Liberals of all stripes believed that somehow there could be reform and amelioration. But practically every thinking person of the late nineteenth century shared with Marx the conviction that capitalist society was a society of inevitable class conflict—and in fact by 1910, most "thinking people," at least in Europe (but also in Japan), were inclining toward Socialism. The greatest of nineteenth-century Conservatives, Benjamin Disraeli (1804–1881), saw capitalist society very much as Marx did. So did his conservative counterpart on the Continent, Otto von Bismarck (1815–1898); it motivated him, after 1880, to enact the social legislation that produced ultimately the twentieth-century Welfare State. One conservative social critic, the nineteenth-century American novelist Henry James, chronicler of American wealth and European aristocracy, was so obsessed by class war and the fear of class war that he made it the theme of his most haunting novel, *The Princess Casamassima*. He was writing it in 1883, the very year of Marx's death.

THE PRODUCTIVITY REVOLUTION

What, then, defeated Marx and Marxism? By 1950, a good many of us already knew that Marxism had failed both morally and economically.* But Marxism was still the one coherent ideology for most of the world, and for most of the world it looked invincible. There were "anti-Marxists" galore, but, as yet, few "non-Marxists," that is, people who thought that Marxism had become irrelevant. Even those bitterly opposed to Socialism were still convinced that it was in the ascendant.†

What, then, overcame the "inevitable contradictions of capitalism," the "alienation" and "immiseration" of the laboring class, and with it the whole notion of the "proletarian"?

The answer is the Productivity Revolution. When knowledge changed its meaning two hundred fifty years ago, it began to be applied to tools, processes, and products. This is still what "technology" means to most people and what is being taught in engineering schools. But two years before Marx's death, the Productivity Revolution had already begun. In 1881, an American, Frederick Winslow Taylor (1856–1915), first applied knowledge to the study of *work*, the analysis of work, and the engineering of work.

Work has been around as long as human beings. All animals in fact have to work for their living. And in the West, the dignity of work has been paid lip service to for a long time. The second oldest Greek text, following the Homeric epics by only a hundred years or so, is a poem by Hesiod (fl. 800 B.C.) entitled *Works and Days*, which sings of the work of the farmer. One of the finest Roman poems is Virgil's (70–19 B.C.) *Georgics*, a cycle of songs about the work of the farmer. Although there is no such concern with work in the Eastern literary tradition, the emperor of China once a year touched a plow to celebrate rice planting.

---

* I had said so already in 1939 in my book *The End of Economic Man*.

† The father of Neo-Conservatism throughout the Western world, the Anglo-Austrian economist Friedrich von Hayek (1899–1992), argued in his *The Road to Serfdom* (1944) that Socialism would inevitably mean enslavement. There was no such thing as "Democratic Socialism"; there was only "totalitarian socialism." But Hayek did not argue in 1944 that Marxism could not work. On the contrary, he was very much afraid that it could and would work. Yet his last book, *The Fatal Conceit* (University of Chicago Press, 1988), written forty years later, argues that Marxism could never have worked. And by the time he published this book, almost everybody—especially in the Communist countries—had already come to the same conclusion.

But in both the West and the East, these were purely symbolic gestures. Neither Hesiod nor Virgil actually studied what a farmer *does*. Nor did anybody else throughout most of recorded history.* Work was beneath the attention of educated people, of well-to-do people, of people of authority. Work was what slaves did. The only way a worker could produce more was by working longer hours or by working harder. Marx himself shared this belief with every other nineteenth-century economist and engineer.

It was pure accident that F. W. Taylor, a well-to-do, educated man, became a worker. Poor eyesight forced him to give up going to Harvard and instead to take a job in an iron foundry. Being extremely gifted, Taylor very soon rose to be one of the bosses. And his metalworking inventions made him a rich man very early. What got Taylor to start on the study of work was his shock at the mutual and growing hatred between capitalists and workers, which had come to dominate the late nineteenth century. Taylor, in other words, saw what Marx saw—and Disraeli and Bismarck and Henry James. But he also saw what they failed to see: that the conflict was unnecessary. He set out to make workers productive so that they would earn decent money.

Taylor's motivation was not efficiency. It was not the creation of profits for the owners. To his very death, he maintained that the major beneficiary of the fruits of productivity had to be the worker, not the owner. His main motivation was the creation of a society in which owners and workers, capitalists and proletarians, could share a common interest in productivity and could build a harmonious relationship on the application of knowledge to work. The people who have come closest to understanding this so far are Japan's post–World War II employers and Japan's post–World War II union leaders.

Few figures in intellectual history have had greater impact than Taylor—and few have been so willfully misunderstood or so

* And there still is no history of work. But then, despite all the philosophizing about knowledge, there is no history of knowledge, either. Both should become important areas of study within the next decades or at least the next century.

assiduously misquoted.* In part, Taylor has suffered because history has proven him right and the intellectuals wrong. In part, he is ignored because contempt for work still lingers, above all among the intellectuals. Surely shoveling sand (the most publicized of Taylor's analyses) is not something an "educated man" would appreciate, let alone consider important.

In much larger part, however, Taylor's reputation has suffered precisely because he applied knowledge to the study of work. This was anathema to the labor unions of his day; and they mounted against Taylor one of the most vicious campaigns of character assassination in American history.

Taylor's crime, in the eyes of the unions, was his assertion that there is no "skilled work." In manual operations, there is only "work." According to Taylor's system of "Scientific Management," all work can be analyzed the same way. Any worker who is then willing to do the work the way analysis shows it should be done is a "first-class man," deserving a "first-class wage"—that is, as much as or more than the skilled worker got with his long years of apprenticeship.

But the unions that were respected and powerful in Taylor's America were the unions in the government-owned arsenals and shipyards in which, prior to World War I, all peacetime defense production was done. These unions were craft monopolies: membership in them was restricted to sons or relatives of members. They required an apprenticeship of five to seven years, but had no systematic training or work study. Nothing was ever allowed to be written down; there were not even blueprints or other drawings of the work to be done. The members were sworn to secrecy and were not permitted to discuss their work with non-members. Taylor's assertion that work could be studied, analyzed, and divided into a series of simple repetitive motions—each of which had to be done in its one right way, its own best time, and with its own right tools—was indeed a frontal attack on them. And so they vilified him and succeeded in having Congress ban any

* In fact, no factually reliable biography was published until 1991, when *Frederick W. Taylor: Myth and Reality* by Charles D. Wrege and Ronald J. Greenwood appeared (Homewood, Ill.: Irwin).

application of "task study" in government arsenals and shipyards—a ban that prevailed until after World War II.

Taylor did not improve matters by offending the owners of his day as much as he offended the unions. While he had little use for unions, he was contemptuously hostile to the owners; his favorite epithet for them was "hogs." And then there was his insistence that the workers rather than the owners should get the lion's share of the revenue gains produced by "Scientific Management." To add insult to injury, his "Fourth Principle" demanded that work study be done in consultation, if not in partnership, with the worker.

Finally, Taylor held that authority in the plant must not be based on ownership. It could be based only on superior knowledge. He demanded, in other words, what we now call "professional management"—and that was anathema and "radical heresy" to nineteenth-century capitalists. He was bitterly attacked by them as a "troublemaker" and a "socialist." (Some of his closest associates, especially Karl Barth, Taylor's right-hand man, were indeed avowed "leftists," and strongly anti-capitalist.)

Taylor's axiom that all manual work, skilled or unskilled, could be analyzed and organized by the application of knowledge seemed preposterous to his contemporaries. And the fact that there was a mystique to craft skill was still universally accepted for many, many years. It was this belief that encouraged Hitler, as late as 1941, to declare war on the United States. For the United States to field an effective force in Europe would require a large fleet to transport troops. America at that time had almost no merchant marine and no destroyers to protect it. Modern warfare, Hitler further argued, required precision optics in large quantities; and there were no skilled optical workers in America.

Hitler was absolutely right. The United States did not have much of a merchant marine, and its destroyers were few and ludicrously obsolete. It also had almost no optical industry. But by applying Taylor's Scientific Management, U.S. industry trained totally unskilled workers, many of them former sharecroppers raised in a pre-industrial environment, and converted them in sixty to ninety days into first-rate welders and ship-builders. Equally, the United States trained the same kind of people within a few months to turn out precision optics of better quality than the Germans ever did—and on an assembly line to boot.

Taylor's greatest impact all told was probably in training. A hundred years before Taylor, Adam Smith had taken for granted that at least fifty years of experience (and more likely a full century) were required for a region to gain the necessary skills to turn out high-quality products—his examples were the production of musical instruments in Bohemia and Saxony, and of silk fabrics in Scotland. Seventy years after Smith, around 1840, a German, August Borsig (1804–1854)—one of the first people outside England to build a steam locomotive—invented the German system of apprenticeship, which combines practical plant experience under a master with theoretical grounding in school. It is still the foundation of Germany's industrial productivity. But even Borsig's apprenticeship took three to five years. Then, first in World War I but above all in World War II, the United States systematically applied Taylor's approach to training "first-class men" in a few months' time. This, more than any other factor, explains why the United States was able to defeat both Japan and Germany.

All the earlier economic powers in modern history—Great Britain, the United States, Germany—emerged through leadership in new technology. The post–World War II economic powers—first Japan, then South Korea, Taiwan, Hong Kong, Singapore—all owe their rise to Taylor's training. It enabled them to endow a still largely pre-industrial and therefore still low-wage work force with world-class productivity in practically no time. In the post–World War II decades, Taylor-based training became the one truly effective engine of economic development.

The application of knowledge to work explosively increased productivity.* For hundreds of years there had been no increase

---

* The term itself was unknown in Taylor's time. In fact, it was still unknown until World War II, when it first began to be used in the United States. As late as 1950, the most authoritative English dictionary, the *Concise Oxford*, still did not list the word "productivity" in its present meaning.

in the ability of workers to turn out goods or to move goods. Machines created greater capacity. But workers themselves were no more productive than they had been in the workshops of ancient Greece, in building the roads of Imperial Rome, or in producing the highly prized woolen cloth which gave Renaissance Florence its wealth.

But within a few years after Taylor began to apply knowledge to work, productivity began to rise at a rate of 3.5 to 4 percent compound a year—which means doubling every eighteen years or so. Since Taylor began, productivity has increased some fiftyfold in all advanced countries. On this unprecedented expansion rest all the increases in both standard of living and quality of life in the developed countries.

Half of this additional productivity has been taken in the form of increased purchasing power; in other words, in the form of a higher standard of living. But between one third and one half has been taken in the form of increased leisure. As late as 1910, workers in developed countries still worked as much as they had ever worked before, that is, at least 3,000 hours a year. Today, the Japanese work 2,000 hours a year, the Americans around 1,850, the Germans at most 1,600—and they all produce fifty times as much per hour as they produced eighty years ago. Other substantial shares of increased productivity have been taken in the form of health care, which has grown from something like zero percent of the gross national product to 8–12 percent in developed countries, and in the form of education, which has grown from around two percent of GNP to 10 percent or more.

Most of this increase—just as Taylor predicted—has been taken by the workers, that is, by Marx's proletarians. Henry Ford (1863–1947) brought out the first cheap automobile, the Model T, in 1907. It was "cheap," however, only by comparison with all other automobiles on the market, which, in terms of average incomes, cost as much as a twin-engine private plane costs today. At $750, Henry Ford's Model T cost what a fully employed industrial worker in the United States earned in three to four years—for 80 cents was then a good day's wage, and of course there were no "benefits." Even an American physician in those years rarely earned more than $500 a year. Today, a unionized automobile worker in the United States, Japan, or Germany, working only forty hours a week, earns $50,000 in wages and benefits—$45,000 after taxes—which is roughly eight times what a cheap new car costs today.

By 1930, Taylor's Scientific Management—despite resistance from unions and from intellectuals—had swept the developed world. As a result, Marx's "proletarian" became a "bourgeois." The blue-collar worker in manufacturing industry, the "proletarian" rather than the "capitalist," became the true beneficiary of Capitalism and Industrial Revolution. This explains the total failure of Marxism in the highly developed countries for which Marx had predicted "revolution" by 1900. It explains why, after 1918, there was no "Proletarian Revolution" even in the defeated countries of Central Europe where there was misery, hunger, and unemployment. It explains why the Great Depression did not lead to a Communist revolution, as Lenin and Stalin—and practically all Marxists—had confidently expected. By that time, Marx's proletarians had not yet become affluent, but they had already become middle class. They had become productive.

"Darwin, Marx, Freud" form the trinity often cited as the "makers of the modern world." Marx would be taken out and replaced by Taylor if there were any justice in the world. But that Taylor is not given his due is a minor matter. It is a serious matter, however, that far too few people realize that the application of knowledge to work created developed economies by setting off the productivity explosion of the last hundred years. Technologists give the credit to machines, economists to capital investment. Yet both were as plentiful in the first hundred years of the capitalist age, before 1880, as they have been since. With respect to technology or to capital, the second hundred years differed very little from the first one hundred. But there was absolutely no increase in worker productivity during the first hundred years—and consequently very little increase in workers' real incomes or any decrease in their working hours. What made the second hundred years so critically different can only be explained as the result of *applying knowledge to work.*

The productivity of the new classes, the classes of the post-capitalist society, can be increased *only* by applying knowledge to work. Neither machines nor capital can do it. Indeed, if applied alone, they are likely to impede rather than to create productivity (as will be discussed further in Chapter 4).

When Taylor started to study work, nine out of every ten working people did manual work, *making or moving things*; in manufacturing, in farming, in mining, in transportation. The productivity of people engaged in making and moving things is still going up at the historical rate of 3.5 to 4 percent—and in American and French agriculture, even faster. But the Productivity Revolution is already over. Forty years ago, in the 1950s, people who engaged in work to make or to move things were still a majority in all developed countries. By 1990, they had shrunk to one fifth of the work force. By 2010 they will form no more than one tenth. Increasing the productivity of manual workers in manufacturing, in farming, in mining, in transportation, can no longer create wealth by itself. The Productivity Revolution has become a victim of its own success. From now on, what matters is the productivity of non-manual workers. And that requires *applying knowledge to knowledge.*

THE MANAGEMENT REVOLUTION

When I decided in 1926 not to go to college but to go to work after finishing secondary school, my father was quite distressed; ours had long been a family of lawyers and doctors. But he did not call me a "dropout." He did not try to change my mind. And he did not prophesy that I would never amount to anything. I was a responsible adult wanting to work as an adult.

Some thirty years later, when my son reached age eighteen, I practically forced him to go to college. Like his father, he wanted to be an adult among adults. Like his father, he felt that in twelve years of sitting on a school bench he had learned little, and that his chances of learning more by spending another four years on a school bench were not particularly great. Like his father at that age, he was action-focused, not learning-focused.

And yet by 1958, thirty-two years after I had moved from high school graduate to trainee in an export firm, a college degree had become a necessity. It had become the passport to careers. Not to go to college in 1958 was "dropping out" for an American boy who had grown up in a well-to-do family and done well in school. My father did not have the slightest difficulty in finding a trainee job for me in a reputable merchant house. Thirty years later, such firms would not have accepted a high school graduate as a trainee; they would all have said, "Go to college for four years—and then you probably should go on to graduate school."

In my father's generation (he was born in 1876), going to college was for the sons of the wealthy and a very small number of poor but exceptionally brilliant youngsters (such as he had been). Of all the American business successes of the nineteenth century, only one went to college: J. P. Morgan went to Göttingen to study mathematics, but dropped out after one year. Few of the others even attended high school, let alone graduated from it.*

By my time, going to college was already desirable; it gave one social status. But it was by no means necessary nor much help in one's life and career. When I did the first study of a major business corporation, General Motors,† the public relations department at the company tried very hard to conceal the fact that a good many of their top executives had gone to college. The proper thing then was to start as a machinist and work one's way up.‡ As late as 1950 or 1960, the quickest route to a middle-class income—in the United States, in Great Britain, in Germany

* In the novels of Edith Wharton, the chronicler of American society around 1910 and 1920, the sons of the old and rich New York families do go to Harvard and to Harvard Law School, but practically none of them then practices law. Higher education was considered a luxury, an ornament, and a pleasant way to spend one's early adulthood.

† Published in *Concept of the Corporation* (1946).

‡ The story is told in the chapter "Alfred P. Sloan" in *Adventures of a Bystander* (1980, reissued 1991).

(though no longer in Japan)—was not to go to college; it was to go to work at age sixteen in one of the unionized mass production industries. There one could earn a middle-class income after a few months—the result of the productivity explosion. Today, these opportunities are practically gone. Now there is practically no access to a middle-class income without a formal degree, which certifies to the acquisition of knowledge that can only be obtained systematically and in a school.

The change in the meaning of knowledge that began two hundred fifty years ago has transformed society and economy. Formal knowledge is seen as both the key personal and the key economic resource. In fact, knowledge is the only meaningful resource today. The traditional "factors of production"—land (i.e., natural resources), labor, and capital—have not disappeared, but they have become secondary. They can be obtained, and obtained easily, provided there is knowledge. And knowledge in this new sense means knowledge as a utility, knowledge as the means to obtain social and economic results.

These developments, whether desirable or not, are responses to an irreversible change: *knowledge is now being applied to knowledge.* This is the third and perhaps the ultimate step in the transformation of knowledge. Supplying knowledge to find out how existing knowledge can best be applied to produce results is, in effect, what we mean by management. But knowledge is now also being applied systematically and purposefully to define what *new* knowledge is needed, whether it is feasible, and what has to be done to make knowledge effective. It is being applied, in other words, to systematic innovation.*

This third change in the dynamics of knowledge can be called the "Management Revolution." Like its two predecessors— knowledge applied to tools, processes, and products, and knowledge applied to human work—the Management Revolution has swept the earth. It took a hundred years, from the middle of the eighteenth century to the middle of the nineteenth century, for the Industrial Revolution to become dominant and worldwide. It

* For more on this, see my *Innovation and Entrepreneurship* (1986).

took some seventy years, from 1880 to the end of World War II, for the Productivity Revolution to become dominant and world-wide. It has taken less than fifty years—from 1945 to 1990—for the Management Revolution to become dominant and worldwide.

Most people when they hear the word "management" still hear "business management." Management did indeed first emerge in its present form in large-scale business organizations. When I began to work on management some fifty years ago, I too concentrated on business management.* But we soon learned that management is needed in all modern organizations. In fact, we soon learned that it is needed even more in organizations that are not businesses, whether not-for-profit but non-governmental organizations (what in this book I propose we call the "social sector") or government agencies. These organizations need management the most precisely because they lack the discipline of the "bottom line" under which business operates. That management is not confined to business was recognized first in the United States. But it is now becoming accepted in every developed country.

We now know that management is a generic function of all organizations, whatever their specific mission. It is the generic organ of the knowledge society.

Management has been around for a very long time. I am often asked whom I consider the best or the greatest executive. My answer is always: "The man who conceived, designed, and built the first Egyptian Pyramid more than four thousand years ago—and it still stands." But management as a specific kind of work was not seen until after World War I—and then by just a handful of people. Management as a discipline only emerged after World War II. As late as 1950, when the World Bank began to lend money for economic development, the word "management" was not even in its vocabulary. In fact, while management was invented thousands of years ago, it was not discovered until after World War II.

---

* In *The Practice of Management*, which first established management as a discipline in 1954, most of the discussion is of business management, and so are most examples.

One reason for its discovery was the experience of World War II itself, and especially the performance of American industry. But perhaps equally important to the general acceptance of management has been the performance of Japan since 1950. Japan was not an "underdeveloped" country after World War II, but its industry and economy were almost totally destroyed, and it had practically no domestic technology. The nation's main resource was its willingness to adopt and adapt the management which the Americans had developed during World War II (and especially training). Within twenty years—from the 1950s, when the American occupation of Japan ended, to the 1970s—Japan became the world's second economic power, and a leader in technology. When the Korean War ended in the early 1950s, South Korea was left even more devastated than Japan had been seven years earlier. And it had never been anything but a backward country, especially as the Japanese systematically suppressed Korean enterprise and higher education during their thirty-five years of occupation. But by using the colleges and universities of the United States to educate their able young people, and by importing and applying the concepts of management, Korea became a highly developed country within twenty-five years.

With this powerful expansion of management came a growing understanding of what management really means. When I first began to study management, during and immediately after World War II, a manager was defined as "someone who is responsible for the work of subordinates." A manager in other words was a "boss," and management was rank and power. This is probably still the definition a good many people have in mind when they speak of "managers" and "management."

But by the early 1950s, the definition of a manager had already changed to one who "is responsible for the performance of people." Today, we know that that is also too narrow a definition. The right definition of a manager is one who "is responsible for the application and performance of knowledge."

This change means that we now see knowledge as the essential resource. Land, labor, and capital are important chiefly as restraints. Without them, even knowledge cannot produce; without them, even management cannot perform. But where there is effective management, that is, application of knowledge to knowledge, we can always obtain the other resources.

That knowledge has become *the* resource, rather than *a* resource, is what makes our society "post-capitalist." This fact changes—fundamentally—the structure of society. It creates new social and economic dynamics. It creates new politics.

FROM KNOWLEDGE TO KNOWLEDGES

Underlying all three phases in the shift to knowledge—the Industrial Revolution, the Productivity Revolution, and the Management Revolution—is a fundamental change in the meaning of knowledge. We have moved from knowledge in the singular to knowledges in the plural.

Traditional knowledge was general. What we now consider knowledge is of necessity highly specialized. We never before spoke of a "man (or woman) of knowledge"; we spoke of an "educated person." Educated people were generalists. They knew enough to talk or write about a good many things, enough to understand a good many things. But they did not know enough to *do* any one thing. As an old saying has it: You would want an educated person as a guest at your dinner table, but you would not want him or her alone with you on a desert island, where you need somebody who knows how to do things. But in today's university the traditional "educated people" are not considered "educated" at all. They are looked down on as dilettantes.

The *Connecticut Yankee at King Arthur's Court*, the hero of the 1889 book by Mark Twain, was not an educated person. He surely knew neither Latin nor Greek, had probably never read Shakespeare, and did not even know the Bible well. But he knew how to do everything mechanical, up to and including generating electricity and building telephones.

The purpose of knowledge for Socrates, as said earlier, was self-knowledge and self-development; results were internal. For his antagonist, Protagoras, the result was the ability to know what to say and to say it well. It was "image," to use a contemporary term. For more than two thousand years, Protagoras's concept of knowledge dominated Western learning and defined knowledge. The medieval *trivium*, the educational system that up to this day underlies what we call a "liberal education," consisted of grammar, logic, and rhetoric—the tools needed to decide what to say and how to say it. They are not tools for deciding *what to do* and how to do it. The Zen concept of knowledge and the Confucian concept of knowledge—the two concepts that dominated Eastern learning and Eastern culture for thousands of years—were similar. The first focused on self-knowledge; the second—like the medieval *trivium*—on the Chinese equivalents of grammar, logic, and rhetoric.

The knowledge we now consider knowledge proves itself in action. What we now mean by knowledge is information effective in action, information focused on results. These results are seen *outside* the person—in society and economy, or in the advancement of knowledge itself.

To accomplish anything, this knowledge has to be highly specialized. This was the reason why the tradition—beginning with the ancients but still persisting in what we call "liberal education"—relegated it to the status of a *technē*, or craft. It could neither be learned nor taught; nor did it imply any general principle whatever. It was specific and specialized—experience rather than learning, training rather than schooling. But today we do not speak of these specialized knowledges as "crafts"; we speak of "disciplines." This is as great a change in intellectual history as any ever recorded.

A discipline converts a "craft" into a methodology—such as engineering, the scientific method, the quantitative method, or the physician's differential diagnosis. Each of these methodologies converts ad hoc experience into system. Each converts anecdote into information. Each converts skill into something that can be taught and learned.

The shift from knowledge to knowledges has given knowledge the power to create a new society. But this society has to be structured on the basis of knowledge as something specialized, and of knowledge people as specialists. This is what gives them their power. But it also raises basic questions—of values, of vision, of beliefs, of all the things that hold society together and give meaning to our lives. As the last chapter of this book will discuss, it also raises a big—and a new—question: what constitutes the educated person in the society of knowledges?

2

The Society of Organizations

A N ORGANIZATION IS A HUMAN GROUP, composed of specialists working together on a common task. Unlike society, community, or family—the traditional social aggregates—organization is purposefully designed and grounded neither in the psychological nature of human beings nor in biological necessity. Yet, while a human creation, it is meant to endure—not perhaps forever, but for a considerable period of time.

An organization is always specialized. It is defined by its task. Community and society, by contrast, are defined by a bond that holds together human beings, whether language, culture, history, or locality. An organization is effective only if it concentrates on one task. The symphony orchestra does not attempt to cure the sick; it plays music. The hospital takes care of the sick but does not attempt to play Beethoven. A mountaineering club set up to climb Himalayan peaks does not look after the homeless in Nepal no matter how great their plight. The school concentrates on teaching and learning, the business on producing and selling goods and services, the church on converting sinners and saving souls, the courts on settling conflicts, the military on fighting wars, the American Heart Association on research into, and prevention of, cardiac degeneration and circulatory disease. Society, community, family *are*; organizations *do*.

"Organization" has become an everyday term. Heads nod when somebody says: "In our organization, everything should revolve around the customer"; or, "All that counts in our organization is meeting the budget"; or, "In this organization, they never forget a mistake you made." Society in all developed countries has become *a society of organizations* in which most, if not all, social tasks are being done in and by an organization: the business enterprise and the labor union; the armed services and the hospital; schools and universities; a host of community services—some of them government agencies, many more (especially in the U.S.) non-profit institutions of the "social sector" (see Chapter 9 below). But there are also symphony orchestras—hundreds of them in the United States—museums and foundations, trade associations and consumer advocates, and so on.

Yet, no one in the United States—or anyplace else—talked of "organizations" until after World War II. Once again the *Concise Oxford*, England's authoritative dictionary, did not list the term in its current meaning in its 1950 edition. Political and social scientists talk of "government" and "business," of "society," "tribe," "community," and "family." But "organization" still has to enter the political, economic, and sociological vocabulary.

This raises three related questions:

- What function do organizations perform? Why are they needed?

- What explains their still being ignored, by and large, in social and political science and in economics?

- Finally, what, precisely, is an organization? How does it work?

THE FUNCTION OF ORGANIZATIONS

The function of organizations is to make knowledges productive. Organizations have become central to society in all

developed countries because of the shift from knowledge to
knowledges.

The more specialized knowledges are, the more effective
they will be. The best radiologists are not the ones who know the
most about medicine; they are the specialists who know how to
obtain images of the body's inside through X-ray, ultrasound,
body scanner, magnetic resonance. The best market researchers
are not those who know the most about business, but the ones who
know the most about market research. Yet neither radiologists
nor market researchers achieve results by themselves; their work
is "input" only. It does not become results unless put together
with the work of other specialists.

Knowledges by themselves are sterile. They become productive only if welded together into a single, unified knowledge. To
make this possible is the task of organization, the reason for its
existence, its function.

We surely overdo specialization these days, worst of all in
Academia. But the cure is not to try to give specialists a "liberal
education" so as to make "generalists" out of them (as I used to
advocate myself for many years). This does not work, we have
now learned. Specialists are effective only as specialists—and
knowledge workers have to be effective. The most highly effective
knowledge workers do not want to be anything but narrow specialists. Neurosurgeons get better and better the more they practice their skill; French horn players do not take up the violin, nor
should they. Specialists need exposure to the universe of knowledge (as will be argued in Chapter 12 below). But they need to
work as specialists, and to concentrate on being specialists. And
for this to produce results, an organization is needed.

ORGANIZATION AS A DISTINCT SPECIES

Why has it taken so long for the scholars to recognize organization, even though it became a predominant social reality decades
ago? The answer tells us a good deal about organization.

It is not surprising that lawyers have not concerned themselves with this new phenomenon. "Organization" is not a legal term any more than are "community" or "society." Nor is "organization" an economic term. Some organizations pursue economic objectives, influence the economy, and are in turn influenced by it, for example, businesses and labor unions. Many others—the churches or the Boy Scouts—are not within the economist's purview. But why have political scientists and sociologists largely ignored a phenomenon that so profoundly affects polity and society?

There is no mention of organizations in the works of the founder of sociology, the Frenchman Auguste Comte (1798–1857). But then there were none in his time. Organization, however, also went unmentioned in the most influential non-Marxist critique of modern society, the 1888 *Gemeinschaft und Gesellschaft* (*Community and Society*), by the German Ferdinand Tönnies (1855–1936), and in the works of the patron saints of modern sociology, the German Max Weber (1864–1920) and the Swiss-Italian Vilfredo Pareto (1848–1923). All three were highly conscious of—and highly critical of—the rise of big business and big unions, but quite oblivious to organization as a new phenomenon. And it is still ignored in more recent social science books.

The explanation is that organization is ignored precisely *because* it profoundly affects both polity and society. Organization is incompatible with what both political and social scientists still assume to be the norm. They still assume that a "normal" society is unitary rather than pluralistic. But the society of organizations is profoundly pluralistic. For organization to be noticed at all by a political scientist or a sociologist, it has to be treated as an abnormality, indeed, a dangerous disease. A good example is *The Legal Foundations of Capitalism* (1924) by the distinguished American labor economist John R. Commons (1862–1945).

Commons argued that the emergence of organization in the form of the business corporation was a poison injected into the American body politic by a "conspiracy" on the part of the late-nineteenth-century Supreme Court, which willfully misinterpreted the Fourteenth Amendment to the Constitution. That this was silly should have been obvious to any reader; every other developed country had accepted corporations without benefit of a Supreme Court or Fourteenth Amendment—indeed, the United States was the last of all developed countries to do so (later even than Japan). Yet Commons made sense to the reader of 1924. Organization was such an aberration that it could only be explained by some sinister conspiracy. The book became a bestseller and one of the bibles of the New Deal "business-bashers" a few years later.

The emergence of organization has been a "paradigm shift," to use a term coined by the American philosopher Thomas Kuhn in his *The Structure of Scientific Revolutions* (1962). It contradicted what political and social scientists *knew* to be the reality. And then, as Kuhn pointed out, it takes between thirty and fifty years—that is, until a new generation has grown up and taken over—before the new reality is perceived, let alone accepted by the scholarly community.

There is still another reason why so little attention has so far been paid to organizations. Armies, churches, universities, hospitals, businesses, labor unions have all been seen, studied, analyzed for a long time and in great detail. But each of them has been treated as unique and *sui generis*. Even now, interviewers are surprised when I tell them that my consulting practice has included all these institutions for more than forty years. Only very recently has it been realized that they all belong to the same species; they are all "organizations." They are the man-made environment, the "social ecology" of post-capitalist society. They have far more in common with one another than they have differences. As I said earlier, most people—and practically everybody outside the United States—still think of "business management" when they hear "management," and do not yet realize that management is a *generic* function pertaining to all organizations alike.* Only the emergence of management since World War II

---

* As pointed out in my *Managing the Non-Profit Organization* (1990), a good many people in the non-profit sector still see churches as churches, hospitals as hospitals, community services as community services, rather than realizing that they all belong to the same family, the non-profits, and the same species, the organization.

has made us perceive that organization is something distinct and discrete. It is neither "community" nor "society" nor "class" nor "family," the modern integrators which social scientists understand. But it is also not "clan" or "tribe" or "kinship group," nor any of the other integrators of traditional society known and studied by anthropologists, ethnographers, and sociologists. Organization is something new and distinct. *But what is it?*

THE CHARACTERISTICS OF ORGANIZATIONS

Organizations are special-purpose institutions. They are effective because they concentrate on *one task*.

If you were to go to the American Lung Association and say: "Ninety percent of all adult Americans [it's always 90 percent, by the way] suffer from ingrown toenails; we need your expertise in research, health education, and prevention to stamp out this dreadful scourge," you'd get the answer: "We are interested only in what lies between the hips and the shoulders."

That explains why the American Lung Association or the American Heart Association or any of the other organizations in the health field get results. Society, community, family have to deal with whatever problem arises. To do so in an organization is "diversification." And in an organization, diversification means splintering. It destroys the performance capacity of any organization—whether business, labor union, school, hospital, community service, or church. Organization is a tool. As with any tool, the more specialized its given task, the greater its performance capacity.

Because the organization is composed of specialists, each with his or her own narrow knowledge area, its mission must be crystal clear. The organization must be single-minded, otherwise its members become confused. They will follow their specialty rather than applying it to the common task. They will each define "results" in terms of that specialty, imposing their own values on the organization. Only a clear, focused, and common mission can hold the organization together and enable it to produce results.

Without such a focused mission, the organization soon loses credibility.

A good example is what happened to American Protestantism in the post–World War II period. Very few strategies have ever been as successful as that of the American Protestant churches when around 1900 they focused their tremendous resources on the social needs of a rapidly industrializing urban society. The doctrine of "Social Christianity" was a major reason why the churches in America did not become marginal, as the churches in Europe did. Yet social action is not the mission of a Christian Church. That is to save souls. Because Social Christianity was so successful, the churches, especially since World War II, have dedicated themselves more and more wholeheartedly to social causes. Ultimately, liberal Protestantism used the trappings of Christianity to further social reform and to promote actual social legislation. Churches became social agencies. They became politicized—and as a result they rapidly lost cohesion, appeal, and members.

The prototype of the modern organization is the symphony orchestra. Each of the two hundred fifty musicians in the orchestra is a specialist, and a high-grade one. Yet by itself the tuba doesn't make music; only the orchestra can do that. The orchestra performs only because all two hundred fifty musicians have the same score. They all subordinate their specialty to a common task. And they all play only one piece of music at any given time.

Results in an organization exist only on the outside. Society, community, family are self-contained and self-sufficient; they exist for their own sake. But all organizations exist to produce results on the outside.

Inside a business, there are only costs. The term "profit center" (which, alas, I myself coined many years ago) is a misnomer. Inside a business, there are only *cost* centers. There are profits only when a customer has bought the product or the service and has paid for it. The result of the hospital is a cured patient, who can go back home (and who fervently hopes never to have to return to the hospital). The results of the school or the university are graduates who put to work what they have learned in their own lives and work. The results of an army are not maneuvers and promotions for generals; they are deterring a war or winning it. The results of the Church are not even on this earth.

This means that results in an organization are always pretty far away from what each member contributes. This is true even in the hospital, where individual contributions—those of the nurse or the physical therapist—are closely related to the result: a cured patient. But many specialists even in the hospital cannot identify their contribution to any particular result. What share in the recovery or rehabilitation of a patient does the X-ray technician have? Or the clinical laboratory technician? Or the dietitian?

In most institutions, the individual's contribution is totally swallowed up by the task and disappears in it. What use is the best engineering department if the company goes bankrupt? And yet, unless the engineering department is first-class, dedicated, and hardworking, the company is likely to go bankrupt. Each member in an organization, in other words, makes a vital contribution (at least in theory) without which there can be no results. But none by himself or herself produces these results.

This then requires, as an absolute prerequisite of an organization's performance, that its task and mission be crystal clear. Results need to be defined clearly and unambiguously—and, if at all possible, measurably.

This also requires that an organization appraise and judge itself and its performance against clear, known, impersonal objectives and goals. Neither society nor community nor family need to set such goals, nor could they. Survival rather than performance is their test.

Joining an organization is always a decision. *De facto* there may be little choice. But even where membership is all but compulsory—as membership in the Christian Church was in Europe for many centuries for all but a handful of Jews and Gypsies—the fiction of a decision to join is carefully maintained. The godfather at the infant's baptism pledges the child's *voluntary* acceptance of membership in the Church.

It may be difficult to leave an organization—the Mafia, for instance, or a Japanese big company, or the Jesuit Order. But it is always possible. And the more an organization becomes an organization of knowledge workers, the easier it is to leave it and move elsewhere (see "The Employee Society" later in this chapter).

Unlike society, community, and family, an organization is therefore always in competition for its most essential resource: qualified, knowledgeable, dedicated people.

This means that organizations have to market membership, fully as much as they market their products and services—and perhaps more. They have to attract people, have to hold people, have to recognize and reward people, have to motivate people, have to serve and satisfy people.

Because modern organization is an organization of knowledge specialists, it has to be an organization of equals, of "colleagues," of "associates." No one knowledge "ranks" higher than another. The position of each is determined by its contribution to the common task rather than by any inherent superiority or inferiority. "Philosophy is the queen of the sciences," says an old tag. But to remove a kidney stone, you want a urologist rather than a logician. The modern organization cannot be an organization of "boss" and "subordinate"; it must be organized as a team of "associates."

An organization is always *managed*. Society, community, family may have "leaders"—and so do organizations. But organizations, and organizations alone, are managed. The managing may be perfunctory and intermittent—as it is, for instance, in the Parent-Teachers Association at a suburban school in the United States, where the elected officers spend only a few hours each year on the organization's affairs. Or management may be a full-time and demanding job for a fairly large group of people, as in the military, the business enterprise, the labor union, the university, and so on. But there have to be people who make decisions, or nothing will ever get done. There have to be people who are accountable for the organization's mission, its spirit, its performance, its results. There must be a "conductor" who controls the "score." There have to be people who focus the organization on its mission, set the strategy to carry it out, and define what the results are. This management has to have considerable authority. Yet its job in the knowledge organization is not to command; it is to direct.

Finally, to be able to perform, an organization must be autonomous. Legally, it may be a government agency, as are Europe's railways, America's state universities, or Japan's leading radio and television network, NHK. Yet in actual operation these organizations must be able to "do their own thing." If they are used to carry out "government policy," they immediately stop performing.

All this, it will be said, is obvious. Yet every one of these characteristics is new, and indeed unique to that new social phenomenon, the organization.

ORGANIZATION AS A DESTABILIZER

Society, community, family are all conserving institutions. They try to maintain stability and to prevent, or at least to slow down, change. But the organization of the post-capitalist society of organizations is a *destabilizer*. Because its function is to put knowledge to work—on tools, processes, and products; on work; on knowledge itself—it must be organized for constant change. It must be organized for innovation; and innovation, as the Austro-American economist Joseph Schumpeter (1883–1950) said, is "creative destruction." It must be organized for systematic abandonment of the established, the customary, the familiar, the comfortable—whether products, services, and processes, human and social relationships, skills, or organizations themselves. It is the very nature of knowledge that it changes fast and that today's certainties will be tomorrow's absurdities.

Skills, in contrast to knowledge, change slowly and infrequently. If Socrates, the stonemason, came back to life today and went to work in a stonemason's yard, the only change of significance would be that he would have to turn out tombstones with a cross on them instead of steles with the symbol of Hermes. The tools are the same even if they now have electric batteries in the handles.* For four hundred years after Gutenberg first used movable type, there was practically no change in the craft of printing—until the steam engine came in, and the discipline of engineering was applied to a *technē*. Throughout history, craftspeople who had learned a trade had acquired everything they would ever need to know during their lifetime after five or six years of apprenticeship, at age seventeen or eighteen. In the post-capitalist society, it is safe to assume that anyone with any knowledge will have to acquire *new* knowledge every four or five years, or else become obsolete.

The changes that most profoundly affect a knowledge do not, as a rule, come out of its own area, as the example of printing shows. The pharmaceutical industry is being profoundly changed today by knowledge that comes out of genetics and biology, disciplines of which few people in a pharmaceutical lab had even heard forty years ago. The greatest challenge to the railroad came not from changes in railroading, but from the automobile, the truck, and the airplane.

Social innovation is as important as new science or new technology in creating new knowledges and in making old ones obsolete. Indeed, social innovation is often more important. What triggered the present worldwide crisis of that proudest of nineteenth-century institutions, the commercial bank, was not the computer or any other technological change. It was the realization that an old but hitherto rather obscure financial instrument, commercial paper, could be used by non-banks to finance companies. This speedily deprived the banks of the business on which they had a monopoly for two hundred years and which gave them most of their income: the commercial loan. The greatest change most probably is that in the last forty years *purposeful*

* A small museum on the Spanish Costa Brava near the ancient city of Emporia exhibits the tools the craftsman of the second and third centuries A.D. used. No craftsman today would have the slightest difficulty figuring out how to use them. He would hardly notice that the tools are two thousand years old.

innovation—both technical and social—has itself become an organized discipline, which is both teachable and learnable.*

Nor is rapid, knowledge-based change confined to business, as is still widely believed. It clearly is needed if the labor union (another of the "success stories" of capitalist society) is to survive. No organization in the fifty years since World War II has changed more than the military, even though uniforms and titles of rank have remained the same. Weapons have changed completely, as the Gulf war of 1991 dramatically demonstrated. Military doctrines and concepts have changed even more drastically. And so have organization structures, command structures, relationships, and responsibilities.

One implication: every organization of today has to build into its very structure *the management of change*.

It has to build in organized abandonment of everything it does. It has to learn to ask every few years of every process, every product, every procedure, every policy: "If we did not do this already, would we go into it now, knowing what we now know?" And if the answer is no, the organization has to ask: "And what do we do now?" It has to *do* something, not just make another study. Increasingly, organizations will have to *plan* abandonment rather than try to prolong the life of a successful policy: practice, or product—something which so far only a few large Japanese companies have faced up to.†

But *the ability to create the new* also has to be built into the organization. Specifically, each organization has to build into its very fabric three systematic practices. First, each organization requires continuing improvement of everything it does—the process the Japanese call *Kaizen*. Every artist throughout history has practiced *Kaizen*, that is, organized, continuous self-improvement. But only the Japanese so far (perhaps because of their Zen tradition) have embodied it in the daily life and work of their business organizations—although not yet into their singu-

* On this, see my *Innovation and Entrepreneurship*.

† On this, see Chapter 24, "The New Japanese Business Strategies," in *Managing for the Future* (1992).

larly change-resistant universities. The aim of *Kaizen* is to improve each product or service so that it becomes a truly different product or service in two or three years' time.

Every organization will secondly have to learn *to exploit*, that is, to develop new applications from its own successes. Again, Japanese businesses have done the best job in this so far, as witness the way in which the Japanese consumer electronics manufacturer has developed one new product after the other out of the same American invention, the tape recorder. But building on their successes is also one of the strengths of the American "pastoral" churches, whose fast growth is beginning to offset the steady decline of both the traditional "Social Christianity" and the traditional fundamentalist churches.

Every organization, third, will have to learn *how to innovate*— and to learn that innovation can and should be organized as a systematic process.

Then of course one comes back to abandonment and the whole process starts all over again.

Unless these tasks are systematically carried out, the knowledge-based post-capitalist organization will very soon find itself obsolescent. It soon will lose performance capacity, and with it the ability to attract and to hold the knowledge specialists on whom it depends.

There is a further implication: post-capitalist society has to be *decentralized*. Its organizations must be able to make fast decisions, based on closeness to performance, closeness to the market, closeness to technology, closeness to the changes in society, environment, and demographics, all of which must be seen and utilized as opportunities for innovation.

Organizations in the post-capitalist society thus constantly upset, disorganize, and destabilize the community. They must change the demand for skills and knowledges. Just when every technical university is geared up to teach physics, geneticists are what we need. Just when the banks have organized credit analysis, they need investment people. Companies on which local communities depend for employment close their factories, or replace grizzled model makers who have spent years learning their craft with twenty-five-year-old "whiz kids" who know computer simulation. Hospitals move the delivery of babies into a freestanding "birthing center" when the knowledge base and technology of obstetrics change. We must be ready to close down a hospital completely when changes in medical practice and technology make a center with fewer than two hundred beds uneconomical and incapable of giving first-rate care. Similarly, for the school or the college to discharge its social function, we must be able to close down a school or a college—no matter how deeply rooted in the local community and how much loved by it—if changes in demographics, technology, or knowledge make a different size or a different philosophy a prerequisite of good performance.

But every one of such changes upsets the community, disrupts it, deprives it of continuity. Every one is perceived as "unfair." Every one destabilizes.

Modern organization creates yet another tension for the community. It has to operate in a community. Its members live in that community, speak its language, send their children to its schools, vote in it, pay taxes to it. They have to feel at home in it—their results are in the community. Yet the organization cannot submerge itself in the community or subordinate itself to that community. Its "culture" has to *transcend* community.

As the American anthropologist Edward T. Hall pointed out in *The Silent Language* (1959), the most important communications in every society are not verbal but cultural, perceived through the way people stand, the way they move, the way they act. Hall showed that a German physician uses quite different signals to get a message across to a German patient from the signals the English, American, or Japanese physician uses. American civil servants would be completely baffled in their own Washington if they were to sit in on the meeting of a local grocery chain discussing next week's advertising promotion. But they easily understand what a Chinese colleague tells them about bureaucratic intrigues in Beijing. And, despite all we hear about differences in "management style," a large Japanese company functions very much like a large American, German, or British company.

It is the nature of the task that determines the culture of an organization, rather than the community in which that task is being performed. Each organization's value system is determined by its task. Every hospital in the world, every school in the world, every business in the world has to believe that what it is doing is an essential contribution to its community and society—the contribution on which all the others in the community depend in the last analysis. To perform its task successfully, it has to be organized and managed the same way. In its culture, the organization thus always transcends the community. If an organization's culture clashes with the values of its community, the organization's culture will prevail—or else the organization will not make its social contribution.

"Knowledge knows no boundaries," says an old proverb. There are as yet very few "transnational" organizations and not even a great many "multinationals." But every knowledge organization is of necessity non-national, non-community. Even if totally embedded in the local community, it is a "rootless cosmopolitan," to use one of Hitler's and Stalin's favorite epithets.

THE EMPLOYEE SOCIETY

Only fifty years ago, the word "employee" was rarely used in English or American, except as a legal term. People then spoke of "capital and labor," or of "management and the worker." The German equivalent, *Mitarbeiter*, was equally uncommon. And when the term was used, it meant low-level clerical people— much like the Spanish *employado* or another German term, *Angestellter*. "Employee" is also an awkward word; it has no clear meaning, and all the equivalents in other languages are equally recent in common usage and equally awkward. The phenomenon itself is so new, we have no proper word for it as yet.

An "employee" is, by definition, somebody who gets paid for working. Yet in the United States, the largest single group of "employees" are people who work without pay. Every second adult American—90 million people all told—works as an unpaid employee for a non-profit organization, most of them giving at least three hours a week of unpaid work.* They are clearly "staff," and consider themselves as such. Yet they are volunteers who receive no pay.

Many people who in effect work as "employees" are not employed in any legal sense. They are "self-employed." A century ago, people who were employed working for somebody else worked for a "master" rather than for an organization or a "boss." There were the factory workers; there were the domestic servants—until World War I vastly outnumbering factory workers in every developed country. There were shop assistants, salespeople, and so on. People with education worked as "independents," by and large. And the largest single group in the 1913 work force in any country (except Great Britain and Belgium) were farmers working for themselves on land they either owned or rented.

Today, farmers are a tiny minority in every developed country; domestic servants have all but disappeared. But the people who sixty or seventy years ago were "independent," that is, the people of education and knowledge, are now employees or "self-employed."

We need a word to describe these people, and we do not have one. In the meantime we may have to do with defining "employees," in the post-capitalist society, as people whose ability to make a contribution depends on their having access to an organization. Whether they are paid is secondary. If these people are "self-employed," they function because they render services to or through organizations: the physician under the British National Health Service; his or her American counterpart working for an "Independent Providers" group; accountants and auditors. These people may not receive a "wage"; they receive a "fee." But their ability to function depends fully as much on their access to an organization as if they were on the payroll.

The higher up we go in terms of income, education, or social status, the more ability to perform and function depends on

---

* On this, see Chapter 9.

access to the organization. Just as post-capitalist society has become a society of organizations, it has also become a society of employees. These are only two different ways to describe the same phenomenon.

As far as the employees who work in subordinate and menial service occupations are concerned—the checkout clerk in the supermarket; the cleaning woman in the hospital; the driver of the delivery truck—their position may not be too different from that of the wage earner, the "worker" of yesterday, whose direct descendants they are. They account for one quarter of the work force, and already outnumber industrial workers. Their position, their productivity, their dignity are central social problems of the post-capitalist society (as will be discussed in Chapter 4).

But the position of the next group, the knowledge workers, is radically different.

Knowledge workers can work only because there is an organization for them to work in. In that respect, they are dependent. But at the same time, they own the "means of production," that is, their knowledge. And knowledge workers account for almost one third of the total work force of a developed country (with skilled service workers accounting for another third or so).

Marx believed that the greatest change in society resulting from the introduction of capitalism was the "alienation" of the worker. The worker no longer owned the tools of production. He could produce only if somebody else, a "capitalist," furnished the tools, especially the steadily more expensive machinery.

The knowledge employee still needs the tools. The capital investment in his or her tools may already be higher than the capital investment in the tools of the manufacturing worker ever was (and the social investment, e.g., in the knowledge worker's education, is of course many times the investment in a manual worker's education). But this capital investment is unproductive unless the knowledge employee brings to bear on it the knowledge which he or she owns and which cannot be taken away.

Machine operators in the factory did as they were told. The machine decided not only what to do but how to do it. The knowledge employee may need a machine, whether it be a computer, an ultrasound analyzer, or a radio telescope. But neither the computer nor the ultrasound analyzer nor the telescope tells the knowledge employee what to do, let alone how to do it. Without this knowledge which is the property of the employee, the machine is unproductive.

The worker under capitalism was totally dependent on the machine. In the employee society, the employee and the tools of production are interdependent. One cannot function without the other. And while the tools of production, such as the ultrasound analyzer, are fixed in place, the technician who knows how to run them and how to interpret their readings has mobility. The machine is dependent on the employee, not the other way around.

Workers throughout history could be "supervised." They could be told what to do, how to do it, how fast to do it, and so on. Knowledge employees cannot, in effect, be supervised. Unless they know more than anybody else in the organization, they are to all intents and purposes useless.

> The marketing manager may tell the market researcher what the company needs to know about the design of a new product and the market segment in which it should be positioned. But it is the market researcher's job to tell the president of the company what market research is needed, how to set it up, and what the results mean. The commanding general of an air base decides how many planes and of what kind are needed for a certain mission. But it is the crew chief, though vastly inferior in rank (and usually not even a commissioned officer), who tells the general how many planes are airworthy and what repairs they need before they can be sent off on their mission. Only a very foolish commanding general overrules his crew chief, despite the difference in rank—and such a commanding general, by the way, will not last very long.

Employees in the employee society need access to an organization. Without it, they cannot produce or perform. And yet they hold a crucial card in their mobility. They carry the means of production—their knowledge—with them.

In the 1980s and 1990s, during the traumatic restructuring of American business, many thousands of knowledge employees lost their jobs. Their company was acquired, merged, spun off, liquidated, and so on. Yet within a very few months, the great majority found new jobs in which to put their knowledge to work. The transition period was painful, and in about half the cases the new job did not pay quite as much as the old one and may not have been as enjoyable. But laid-off technicians, professionals, and managers found that they had the "capital"—their knowledge; they owned the *means* of production. Somebody else, the organization, had the *tools* of production. The two needed each other. By itself, neither was capable of producing. Neither, in other words, is "dependent" or "independent." They are interdependent.

> Japan officially still believes in lifetime commitment, especially for knowledge employees, professionals, managers, and technicians. But the great scandal of Japan in 1989 was the "Recruit Affair," in which a rapidly growing publisher, Recruit, bribed politicians by giving them free shares. What made these Recruit shares so attractive? What made Recruit so extraordinarily profitable? The company publishes magazines for technicians, professionals, and middle managers who look for better jobs than they presently have. These magazines contain nothing but job offers for such people. When riding on the Tokyo subway, the foreigner is told, older people read adult comics; but younger people read the magazines which offer positions for knowledge employees already employed by other companies. Even in Japan, the knowledge employee is rapidly gaining mobility, despite all the emphasis on "loyalty" and "lifetime commitment."

"Loyalty" from now on cannot be obtained by the paycheck; it will have to be earned by proving to knowledge employees that the organization which presently employs them can offer them exceptional opportunities to be effective. Not so long ago, we talked about "labor"; increasingly, now, we are talking of "human resources." This implies that it is the individual knowledge employee who decides in large measure what he or she will contribute, and how great the yield from his or her knowledge can or should be.

* * *

But in the knowledge society, even low-skilled service workers are not "proletarians." Collectively, the employees own the means of production. Individually, few of them are wealthy. Even fewer of them are rich (though a good many are financially independent—what we now call "affluent"). Collectively, however, whether through their pension funds, through mutual funds, through their retirement accounts, and so on, they own the means of production. The people who exercise the voting power for the employees are themselves employees; take, for example, the civil servants who manage the pension funds of state and local governments in the United States. These pension fund managers are the only true "capitalists" in the United States. The "capitalists" have thus themselves become employees in the post-capitalist knowledge society. They are paid as employees; they think as employees; they see themselves as employees. But they act as capitalists.

One implication is that capital now serves the employee, where under Capitalism the employee served capital. But a second implication is that we now have to redefine the role, power, and function of both capital and ownership. As we shall see in the next chapter, we have to rethink *the governance of corporations.*

3

Labor, Capital, and Their Future

I F KNOWLEDGE IS *the* resource of post-capitalist society, what then will be the future role and function of the two key resources of capitalist (and socialist) society, labor and capital?

Socially, the new challenges (to be discussed in Chapters 4 and 5 and in the last part of this book) will predominate. And the success of post-capitalist society will largely depend on our answers to them. But politically, the unfinished business of capitalist society will be highly visible: the disappearance of labor as a factor of production, and the redefinition of the role and function of traditional capital.

We have moved already into an "employee society" where labor is no longer an asset. We equally have moved into a "capitalism" without capitalists—which defies everything still considered self-evident truth, if not "the laws of nature," by politicians, lawyers, economists, journalists, labor leaders, business leaders; in short, by most everybody regardless of political persuasion. For that reason, these issues will be in the *political* spotlight in the decades ahead. To be able to tackle successfully the new challenges of this transition period, we must resolve these two items of unfinished business: the future role and function of labor, and the future role and function of money capital.

IS LABOR STILL AN ASSET?

American manufacturing production remained almost unchanged as a percentage of gross national product in the years of the "manufacturing decline." It stood at 22 percent of GNP in 1975, and at 23 percent in 1990. During those twenty years, gross national product increased two and a half times. In other words, total American manufacturing production grew more than two and a half times in those twenty years.

But manufacturing employment did not increase at all. On the contrary, manufacturing employment went down from 1960 to 1990 as a percentage of the work force and even in absolute numbers. It fell by almost half in these thirty years, from 25 percent of the total labor force in 1960 to 16 or 17 percent in 1990. During this time, the total American work force doubled— the largest increase ever recorded by any country in peacetime. All the increase was, however, in jobs other than making and moving things.

These trends are certain to continue. Unless there is a severe depression, manufacturing production in America is likely to stay at about the same 23 percent of gross national product, which, for the next ten or fifteen years, should mean another near doubling. During the same period, however, employment in manufacturing is likely to fall to 12 percent or less of the total labor force. That would mean a further fairly sharp shrinkage of the total number of people employed in manufacturing work.

The development in Japan is almost identical. There, too, total manufacturing production has increased two and a half times in the twenty years between 1970 and 1990. There, too, however, manufacturing employment in total numbers has not increased at all. And there too, from now on, even a sizable increase in manufacturing production will not be sufficient to offset the steady shrinkage in manufacturing jobs. In Japan, too, by the year 2000 total employment in manufacturing will be substantially less than it was in 1990.

The response of these two countries to identical developments is, however, completely different. In the United States, there is gloom about the "decline of American manufacturing," if not panic about the "death of American manufacturing." In the United States, manufacturing is equated with blue-collar employment. In Japan, the reaction has been the opposite. What matters to the Japanese is the increase in manufacturing *production.* Japan sees the trends of the last twenty years as victory; America sees them as defeat. Japan sees the glass as "half full"; America as "half empty."

As a result of these differences in attitude, the policies of the two countries also differ radically. Every state, county, and city in America is desperately trying to attract manufacturers who offer blue-collar jobs. Poor rural states like Kentucky and Tennessee have lured Japanese automobile manufacturers with offers of long-range tax benefits and low-interest loans. The city of Los Angeles in early 1992 awarded a multi-*billion*-dollar contract for rapid-transit equipment to the company that promised to create all of ninety-seven manufacturing jobs in a region that has almost 15 million inhabitants!

By contrast, Japanese companies are moving manual work in manufacturing out of Japan as fast as they can—into the United States; into plants at the U.S.-Mexican border; into Indonesia.

In the United States, manufacturing jobs are seen as a priceless asset. In Japan, they are more and more seen as a liability.

Differences in social structure between the two countries explain, in part, these different reactions to the same trends. The shrinkage of manual jobs in making and moving things is above all a threat to America's most visible minority, the blacks. Their biggest economic gains during the last thirty years have come from moving into well-paid jobs in unionized mass production industries. In all other areas of economy and society black gains have been much more modest. The shrinkage of jobs in the unionized mass production industries therefore aggravates what all along has been America's most serious problem—all the more daunting since it is as much a problem of conscience as it is a social problem.

In Japan, practically all young people now get a high school degree, and then are considered overqualified for manual work. They become clerical workers. Those who go on to the university—and the same proportion of young males goes to the university in Japan as in the United States—take managerial or professional jobs only. If Japan were not able to cut down on the number of manual jobs in manufacturing, it would face an extreme labor shortage. In other words, the shrinkage in manufacturing jobs is the answer to a problem for the Japanese.

A country needs a manufacturing base, so Americans would argue—and most Europeans as well. This means manufacturing jobs. But the Japanese argue—convincingly—that the supply of young people in the developing countries qualified for nothing but manual work in manufacturing is so large—and will remain so large for at least another thirty years—that worrying about the "industrial base" is nonsense. A country that has the knowledge workers to design products and to market them will have no difficulty getting those products made at low cost and high quality. In fact, the Japanese argue that to encourage blue-collar manual work in making and moving things *weakens* a developed economy. In a developed economy, even people who learn little in school represent a tremendous educational investment. Employed as manufacturing workers, such people yield only a pitiful return to society and economy, perhaps no more than 1 or 2 percent. Yet people in developing countries who have had no schooling are fully as productive after a little training as any manual worker in the most highly developed country. Economically as well as socially, it would be much more productive—the Japanese argue—to put the money spent to create blue-collar jobs in developed countries instead into advancing the country's education, and thus to ensure that youngsters learn enough to become qualified for knowledge work, or at least for high-level service work.

HOW MUCH LABOR IS NEEDED—AND WHAT KIND?

A developed country does indeed need a manufacturing base. Yet the facts support the Japanese position. The United States still has the world's strongest agricultural base, even though farmers now constitute only 3 percent of the working population (they still formed 25 percent at the end of World War II). The United States equally could still be the world's largest manufacturer, with manufacturing workers constituting no more than 10 percent (or less) of the working population.

In 1980, United States Steel, America's largest integrated steel company, employed 120,000 people in steel production. Ten years later, it employed 20,000 people in steel production, and yet produced almost the same steel tonnage. Within ten years the productivity of the manual worker engaged in steelmaking had increased seven-fold. A large part of the increase was obtained by closing down old, outmoded plants. Another large part of the increase came from investment in new equipment. But the lion's share of the jump in productivity represents the results of re-engineering work flow and tasks.

As a result, U.S. Steel's best mills are now the world's most productive *integrated* steelmakers. And yet, like all integrated steel mills the world over, they are still grossly overstaffed. And America's integrated steel mills are still losing money. The so-called minimills (in 1991, almost one third of all steel produced in the U.S. was produced by minimills) are again three to four times as productive as the most productive integrated mill. The best of American minimills could probably produce as much steel as U.S. Steel does with not much more than one sixth of U.S. Steel's present employment. And increasingly the minimills can turn out all the products an integrated steel mill produces and of the same quality. Admittedly, a minimill obtains these results by not having to perform the most labor-intensive operations in an integrated steel mill. It does not smelt iron ore to obtain iron; nor does it convert iron into steel. It starts with scrap steel. But for the foreseeable future, the world will have abundant supplies of scrap steel.

It is not the process that is the main difference between the integrated steel mill and the minimill. Workers in the minimill are not blue-collar workers making and moving things; they are knowledge workers. The minimill changes steelmaking from applying muscle and skill to work to applying knowledge to work: knowledge of the process; of chemistry; of metallurgy; of computer operations. The workers whom U.S. Steel laid off need not apply at the minimill.

This is an extreme example, to be sure. But it indicates the general direction.

Plenty of people will always be needed who can bring only muscle to the job. With our present knowledge of training, they can quickly be made productive in traditional jobs. Even more people will be needed who can only bring manual skills to the job. But the greatest employment need of the next decades will be for "technicians."

Technicians not only need a high level of skill; they also need a high degree of formal knowledge, and above all a high capacity to learn and to acquire additional knowledge. Technicians are not the successors to yesterday's blue-collar workers. They are basically the successors to yesterday's highly skilled workers; or rather, they are highly skilled workers who now also possess a substantial amount of formal knowledge, formal education, and the capacity for continuous learning.

A hot dispute is raging today in Academia and among policy makers: Is it a sufficient "manufacturing base" for developed countries to have their businesses carry on at home the work on technology, design, and marketing of industrial products, or do they also have to manufacture at home? The question is moot. If a country has the knowledge base, it will also manufacture. But this manufacturing work will not be competitive if carried out by traditional blue-collar workers who serve the machine. In competitive manufacturing, the work will largely be done by knowledge workers whom the machine serves—as computer consoles and computerized work stations serve the ninety-seven technicians in a steelmaking minimill.

This will create tremendous problems for *developing* countries. They can no longer expect to be able to obtain large numbers of manufacturing jobs by training low-wage people. Manual labor, no matter how cheap, will not be able to compete with knowledge labor, no matter how well paid. But this also creates tremendous problems for countries—the United States is the prime example—in which there are large groups of "minority" people who are "developing" rather than "developed" in their educational qualifications. The United Kingdom in its old working-class enclaves in the north, in Scotland (especially along the Clyde), and in Northern Ireland faces a similar problem of a working-class culture which in effect is the culture of a developing rather than a developed country. On the continent of Europe, too, despite an educational system with relatively open access, the trend toward labor becoming a liability rather than an asset will, for a fairly long transition period, create both serious social problems and political conflicts.

Everywhere this trend also raises difficult and highly emotional questions about the role, function, and future of this century's most successful organization, the labor union.

To maintain and strengthen a country's manufacturing base and to ensure that it remains competitive surely deserves high priority. But this means accepting that manual labor in making and moving things is rapidly becoming a liability rather than an asset. Knowledge has become the key resource for all work. Creating traditional manufacturing jobs—as the Americans, the British, and the Europeans are still doing—is at best a short-lived expedient. It may actually make things worse. The only long-term policy which promises success is for developed countries *to convert manufacturing from being labor based into being knowledge based.*

CAPITALISM WITHOUT CAPITALISTS

Never before have there been such enormous pools of money as are now held in developed countries by institutional investors, primarily pension funds. In the United States, where the development started and has gone furthest, the biggest pension fund holds assets of $80 billion; even a small pension fund may have something like $1 billion invested in the economy. These pools of capital dwarf anything the greatest "capitalist" of past times commanded. The age structure of a developed society virtually guarantees that the pension funds will become more important in every single developed country.

This is an unprecedented development, that began only in the 1950s.* It is so new, in fact, that the management and regulation of the pension funds have still to be worked out.

How to protect such enormous pools of money against looters is one big problem. In the United States, the pension funds of private businesses do have some protection: it would not have been easy to loot pension funds in America the way Robert Maxwell, the late British newspaper magnate, looted the pension funds of his British newspapers in 1990 and 1991. But even in the United States, the safeguards are woefully inadequate. And no safeguards at all exist against the most serious danger: the looting for political purposes of the pension funds of government employees. In fact, in the United States the pension funds of public employees—of New York City, New York State, Philadelphia, the state of California, and so on—have regularly been misused to plug holes in the budgets of states and cities.

Equally great is the danger that special-interest groups, such as labor unions, will use their political power to divert pension fund money to subsidize themselves—usually under the fraudulent pretext of making pension fund money serve "socially constructive purposes." Pension funds are the savings of today's employees. They must not serve anything or anyone except the financial future of the present employees. This is the greatest "social purpose" they can possibly have.

* It was first seen and analyzed in *The Unseen Revolution* (1976), soon to be reissued by Transaction Publishers, New Brunswick, N.J., under the title *The Pension Fund Revolution*.

THE PENSION FUND AND ITS OWNERS

To integrate the pension funds' real owners, present employees and future pensioners, into the management of the pension fund is a challenge that has not so far been tackled in any country. At present, the only relationship these owners have is their expectation of a check in the future. Yet, for most people over forty-five in developed countries, the stake in the pension fund is their largest single asset. During the nineteenth century, the biggest financial need of common people was for life insurance to protect their families in the event of their early death. With life expectancies now almost double those of the nineteenth century, the biggest need of common people today is protection against the threat of living too long. The nineteenth-century "life insurance" was really "death insurance." The pension fund is "old-age" insurance. It is an essential institution in a society in which most people can expect to outlive their working lives by many years.

The regulation of pension funds, and their protection against looting, will remain a challenge to policy makers and lawmakers for years to come. In all likelihood, the challenge will only be met after we have had a few nasty scandals. Similarly, the integration of the real owners into the pension fund structure will require years of debate, of experimentation, of "scandals."

The proper management of the pension funds and their integrity will also be a major public issue—and deservedly so. But this issue does not primarily concern us here. Our concern is with *the role and function of capital* now that institutional investors, and especially the pension funds, are rapidly becoming the major sources of capital in developed countries. In the United States at the end of 1992, institutional investors held at least 50 percent of the share capital of large corporations. They also held an almost equal proportion of the fixed debt even of America's medium-sized—let alone large—businesses, whether publicly or privately owned. And the one hundred largest pension funds held something like one third of all pension fund assets at the end of 1992.

No such concentration of financial control has ever existed in the United States before; in fact, it would never have been allowed.

Historically, the United States has always had the lowest concentration of financial power. In Germany, for at least a century, a very few large banks have controlled (either directly or through shares held by them for their customers) something like three fifths of the voting power in large and even in middle-sized companies. In Japan, the *Keiretsu* (the groups formed around a bank or a trading company such as Mitsubishi, Mitsui, or Sumitomo) have traditionally controlled the majority of Japan's large businesses. Italy, similarly, has an extremely high concentration in which financial power and control are shared—partly in competition and partly in cooperation—between a very small number of highly concentrated private groups and an equally small number of government consortia controlled by and beholden to political parties.

For the United States, however, the concentration of capital in the institutional investors is unprecedented. Yet it is the U.S. development that is likely to become the model. The traditional way in which financial power was concentrated in Japan and Europe will not survive the rise of the pension fund. And the traditional institutions in which financial power has been concentrated are most unlikely to be able to extend their control to the new pension funds. Different countries will undoubtedly structure the pension fund economy their own way, just as they structured the "finance capitalism" which emerged in the closing years of the nineteenth century. But pension fund capitalism will become the universal ownership mode in developed countries; the age structure of developed countries alone makes this practically inevitable.

Pension fund capitalism is fundamentally as different from any earlier form of capitalism as it is from anything any socialist ever envisaged as a socialist economy.

Pension funds are a curious and indeed paradoxical phenomenon. They are "investors" who control huge pools of capital and its investment. But neither the managers who run them nor their owners are "capitalists." Pension fund capitalism is capitalism *sans* the capitalists.

Legally, pension funds are "owners"; but only legally. In the first place, the pension funds are "trustees." The owners, the future pensioners, are the ultimate beneficiaries. And the pension funds are themselves managed by employees such as financial analysts, portfolio managers, actuaries. These are well-paid professionals, but unlikely to be rich themselves. Indeed, the largest of the American pension funds, the pension funds of the employees of the federal government, of the states, and of the cities, are managed by civil servants who are being paid as such.

Pension fund capitalism is also capitalism without "capital." The money of the pension funds—and of their siblings, the mutual funds—does not fit any known definition of capital; and this is not just a matter of semantics. Actually, the funds of the pension funds are deferred wages. They are being accumulated to provide the equivalent of wage income to people who no longer work.

According to Marx, in the definition of capital that was accepted by large majorities of people throughout the nineteenth and early twentieth centuries, all capital is accumulated through expropriation of the wage earner. "Property is theft," proclaimed an early Socialist classic. Obviously this definition does not fit the capital of the pension funds, in which the wage earners remain the owners of the money.

But the capital of the pension funds also does not fit any non-Marxist definition of capital. In pension fund capitalism, the wage earners finance their own employment by deferring part of their wages. Wage earners are the main beneficiaries of the earnings of capital and of capital gains. We have no social, political, or economic theory that fits what has already become reality.

THE GOVERNANCE OF CORPORATIONS

The most important question raised by the emergence of the pension funds (and of the other institutional investors) as the main suppliers of capital and the majority owners of the large businesses is their role and function in the economy. Their emergence makes obsolete all traditional ways of managing and controlling the large business. It forces us to think through and redefine *the governance of corporations.*

One of the most influential American books of this century, *The Modern Corporation and Private Property* by Adolph A. Berle and Gardner Means, was published in 1933. It pointed out that in a large corporation, the legal owners, the shareholders, were no longer able or willing to control. Professional management controlled without ownership stake. There was no other way, Berle and Means showed, to finance the large corporation. It had outgrown financing by any single owner or group of owners. Instead, it required financing through the investments of large numbers of people, not one of whom could possibly own enough to control the company or even to be much concerned about its management. "Property," Berle and Means maintained, had become "investment." To whom, therefore, is management accountable, they asked? And for what?

Twenty years later, an attempt was made in the United States to answer these questions. The attempted answer—developed around 1950 (and first critically discussed in 1954 in my book *The Practice of Management*)—was that management is a "trustee," accountable to no one single group or person. "Management" in the large publicly owned company should act in the "best balanced interests" of a number of constituencies: shareholders, employees, suppliers, plant communities, and so on—what are now called "stakeholders." Management would discharge its duties by being a benevolent despot. As in all benevolent despotisms, no one tried to define what those "best balanced interests" were or should be, let alone how performance of this "trusteeship" could be defined or measured. Worse still, there was no attempt to make management accountable to anyone. On the contrary, boards of directors—legally the governing organ of a corporation—became increasingly impotent rubber stamps for a company's top management.

Any government, whether that of a company or a nation,

degenerates into mediocrity and malperformance if it is not clearly accountable to someone for results. This is what happened to the big American corporation in the thirty years between 1950 and 1980.

This development then made possible the frantic financial manipulations of the 1970s and 1980s: the hostile takeovers, the leveraged buyouts, the acquisitions, and the divestments. It made possible the decade of greed and the "bubble economy," which predictably collapsed in a series of financial scandals. But hostile takeovers and leveraged buyouts were possible only because in the meantime institutional investors had emerged as the holders of controlling majorities in the large corporations. It was the institutional investors who financed the raiders. As trustees, the institutional investors were legally obligated to support the raiders if they offered—or seemed to offer—a little more money for shares held by the pension fund than the current stock market price.

What emerged from this frantic decade was a redefinition of the purpose and rationale of big business and of the function of management. Instead of being managed "in the best balanced interests of stakeholders," corporations were now to be managed exclusively to "maximize shareholder's value."

This will not work, either. It forces the corporation to be managed for the shortest term. But that means damaging, if not destroying, the wealth-producing capacity of the business. It means decline, and fairly swift decline. Long-term results cannot be achieved by piling short-term results on short-term results. They should be achieved by balancing short-term and long-term needs and objectives. Furthermore, managing a business exclusively for the shareholders alienates the very people on whose motivation and dedication the modern business depends: the knowledge workers. An engineer will not be motivated to work to make a speculator rich.

The "professional managers" of the 1930s were right in asserting that a business has to be managed by balancing short-term and long-term results, and by balancing the interests of different constituencies, each with a genuine stake in the business. But we also now know, as we did not know forty years ago, how to do this. In fact, we know in what areas to set objectives, and how to integrate the pursuit of goals in different areas into a focused strategy. We now know how to integrate business results and financial results. We now know that in a modern economy, an economy of change and innovation, there is no such thing as "profit." There are only costs: costs of the past (which the accountant records) and costs of an uncertain future. And the minimum financial return from the operations of the past that is adequate to the costs of the future is the cost of capital. By this measurement, incidentally, all but a handful of American companies have failed to cover their costs in the last thirty years.

MAKING MANAGEMENT ACCOUNTABLE

In other words, we now know *what* management should be accountable for. But to whom should it be accountable? The standard answer is, of course, to "the owners," and this would then mean the institutional investors and especially the pension funds.

But as we have already seen, the pension funds cannot possibly act as "owners." They cannot possibly manage a business. Yet they also can no longer consider themselves as "investors." An investor can always sell his holdings. But the holdings of large pension funds—even of medium-sized ones—are so big that they simply cannot be sold. The only market for them is other pension funds. Pension funds, in other words, can neither manage a business nor walk away from it. *They have to make sure that the business is being managed.*

We therefore can predict with high probability that within the next twenty years we are going to develop what I have been calling a "business audit." It will track the performance of a company and its management against a strategic plan and specific objectives. This will then show, over a period of a few years, whether a business is performing well or not. The first steps in the direction of developing such a business audit and the institutions to administer it are already being taken. The models are the public accountants who in all developed countries routinely inspect and audit the financial performance of a business. Such a business audit will give management the autonomy it needs to perform. It will also establish accountability for performance, *and enforce it*. For it will put management under the discipline of known and public performance requirements. At the same time the business audit will enable the trustees of capital, the institutional investors, to act as responsible owners, whose duty it is to take care of the property in their keeping, of the companies whose legal owners they represent: the future beneficiaries of the pension fund. The interests of these beneficiaries are, of course, in long-term rather than short-term results, and in the growth of the economy rather than in short-term stock market prices.

This role and function are totally different in theory as well as in practice from that which capital had in "capitalism." The function of capital will increasingly be to make knowledge *effective in performance*. It will increasingly have to serve performing management rather than to dominate it.

And what should this new social structure be called? When I first discussed it, in the mid-seventies, I called it "pension fund socialism." Might "employee capitalism" be a better term?

4

The Productivity of the
New Work Forces

THE NEW CHALLENGE facing the post-capitalist society is the productivity of knowledge workers and service workers. To improve the productivity of knowledge workers will in fact require drastic changes in the structure of the organizations of post-capitalist society, and in the structure of society itself.

Forty years ago, people doing knowledge work and service work formed still less than one third of the work force. Today, such people account for three quarters if not four fifths of the work force in all developed countries—and their share is still going up. Their productivity, rather than the productivity of the people who make and move things, is *the* productivity of a developed economy. It is abysmally low. The productivity of people doing knowledge work and service work may actually be going down rather than going up. One third of the capital investment in developed countries in the last thirty years has gone into equipment to handle data and information, computers, fax machines, electronic mail, closed-circuit television, and so on. Yet the number of people doing clerical work, that is, the number of people to whose work most of this equipment is dedicated, has been going up much faster than total output or gross national product. Instead of becoming more productive, clerical workers have become less productive. The same is true of salespeople and also of engineers. And no one, I dare say, would maintain that the teacher of 1990 is more productive than the teacher of 1900 or the teacher of 1930.

The lowest level of productivity occurs in government employment. And yet governments everyplace are the largest employers of service workers. In the United States, for instance, one fifth of the entire work force is employed by federal, state, and local governments, predominantly in routine clerical work. In the United Kingdom, the proportion is roughly one third. In all developed countries, government employees account for a similar share of the total work force.

Unless we can learn how to increase the productivity of knowledge workers and service workers, and increase it fast, the developed countries will face economic stagnation and severe social tension. People can only get paid in accordance with their productivity. Their productivity creates the pool of wealth from which wages and salaries are then paid. If productivity does not go up, let alone if it declines, higher *real* incomes cannot be paid.

Knowledge workers are likely to be able to command good incomes, regardless of their productivity or the productivity of the total economy. They are in a minority; and they have mobility. But even knowledge workers, in the long run, must suffer a decline in real income unless their productivity goes up. Large numbers of service workers perform work that demands fairly low skills and relatively little education. If an economy in which service worker productivity is low tries to pay them wages considerably above what their productivity produces, inflation must erode everybody's real income. In the not so long run, inflation will then also create serious social tensions. If service workers, however, are paid only according to their productivity, the gap between their income and that of the "privileged," that is, the knowledge workers, must steadily widen—again creating severe social tensions.

A good deal of service work does not differ too much from the work of making and doing things. This includes such clerical jobs as data processing, billing, answering customers' inquiries, handling insurance claims, issuing drivers' licenses to motorists—in fact, about two thirds of all the work done in government offices, and about one third or more of all the clerical and services work done in businesses, in universities, in hospitals, and so on. This is in effect "production work," which differs from the work done in the factory only in that it is being done in an office. But even this work has first to be "re-engineered" before it can be made productive. It has to be studied and restructured for optimum contribution and achievement. In all other work done by the new work forces, both knowledge workers and service workers, raising productivity requires new concepts and new approaches.

In the work on productivity in making and moving things, the task is given and determined. When Frederick W. Taylor started to study the shoveling of sand, he could take it for granted that the sand had to be shoveled. In a good deal of the work of making and moving things, the task is actually "machine-paced": the individual worker serves the machine.

In knowledge work, and in practically all service work, the machine serves the worker. The task is not given; it has to be determined. The question, "What are the expected results from this work?" is almost never raised in traditional work study and Scientific Management. But it is the key question in making knowledge workers and service workers productive. And it is a question that demands risky decisions. There is usually no right answer; there are choices instead. And results have to be clearly specified, if productivity is to be achieved.

WHAT KIND OF TEAM?

There is a second major difference between the productivity of making and moving things and the productivity of knowledge work and service work. In knowledge and service work, we have to decide how the work should be organized. What kind of human team is appropriate for this kind of work and its flow?

Most human work is carried out in teams; hermits are exceedingly rare. Even the most solitary artists, writers, or painters, depend on others for their work to become effective—the writer on an editor, a printer, a bookstore; the painter on a gallery to sell his or her work; and so on. And most of us work in far closer relationship to our teammates.

There is a great deal of talk today about "creating teamwork." This is largely a misunderstanding. It assumes that the existing organization is not a team organization, and that is demonstrably false. It secondly assumes that there is only one kind of team; but in effect there are three major kinds of teams for all human work. And for work to be productive, it has to be organized into the team that is appropriate to the work itself, and its flow.*

The first kind of team is exemplified by the baseball or cricket team; it is also the kind of team that operates on a patient in the hospital. In this team, all players play *on* the team but they do not play *as* a team.

> Each player on a baseball or a cricket team has a fixed position which he never leaves. In baseball, the outfielders never assist each other. They will stay in their respective positions. "If you are up at bat, you are totally alone," is an old baseball saying. Similarly, the anesthesiologist will not come to the assistance of the surgical nurse or the surgeon.

This team does not enjoy a good press today. In fact, when people talk about "building teams," they usually mean that they want to move away from this kind of team. Yet the baseball—or cricket—team has great strengths that should not be discounted. Because all players occupy fixed positions, they can be given specific tasks of their own, can be measured by performance

* On various teams, and especially on the analogy between teams in business and teams in sports, see Robert W. Keidel, *Game Plans* (New York: E. P. Dutton, 1985).

scores for each task, can be trained for each task. It is by no means accidental that in both baseball and cricket there are statistics on every player, going back for decades. The surgical team in the hospital functions much the same way.

For repetitive tasks and for work in which the rules are well known, the baseball team is the ideal. And it was this model on which modern mass production—the work of making and moving things—was organized, and to which it owes a great deal of its performance capacity.

The second type of team is the soccer team. It is also the team concept on which the symphony orchestra is organized, and the model for the hospital team that rallies around the patient who goes into cardiac arrest at two in the morning.

> On this team, too, all players have fixed positions. The tuba players in the orchestra will not take over the parts of the double basses. They stick to their tubas. In the crisis team at the hospital, the respiratory technician will not make an incision in the chest of the patient to massage the heart. But on these teams, the members work *as* a team. Each coordinates his or her part with the rest of the team.

This team requires a conductor or a coach. And the word of the conductor or coach is law. It also requires a "score." And it requires endless rehearsals to work well. But, unlike the baseball team, it has great flexibility if the score is clear and if the team is well led. And it can move very fast.

Finally, there is the doubles tennis team—the team also of the jazz combo or of the four or five senior executives who together constitute the "President's Office" in the large American company, or the *Vorstand* (board of management) in the German company.*

> This team has to be small—seven to nine people may be the maximum. The players have a "preferred" rather than a "fixed" position; they "cover" for one another. And they adjust them-

---

* On this, see also the discussion of the top management job in my *Management: Tasks, Responsibilities, Practices* (1973).

selves to the strengths and weaknesses of each other. The player in the back court in doubles tennis adjusts to the strengths and weaknesses of the partner who plays the net. And the team only functions when this adjustment to the strengths and weaknesses of the partners has become conditioned reflex, that is, when the player in the back court starts running to "cover" for the weak backhand of the partner at the net the moment the ball leaves the racket of the player on the other side.

A well-calibrated team of this kind is the strongest team of all. Its total performance is greater than the sum of the individual performances of its members, for this team uses the strength of each member while minimizing the weaknesses of each. But this team requires enormous self-discipline. The members have to work together for a long time before they actually function as a "team."

These three types of teams cannot be mixed. One cannot play baseball and soccer with the same team on the same field at the same time. The symphony orchestra cannot play the way a jazz combo plays. The three teams must also be "pure"; they cannot be hybrids. And to change from one team to another is exceedingly difficult and painful. The change cuts across old, long-established, and cherished human relationships. Yet any major change in the nature of the work, its tools, its flow, and its end product may require changing the team.

This is particularly true with respect to any change in the *flow of information*.

In the baseball-type team, players get their information from the situation. Each receives information appropriate to his or her task, and receives it independently of the information the teammates all receive. In the symphony orchestra or the soccer team, the information comes largely from conductor or coach. They control the "score." In the doubles tennis team, the players get their information largely from each other. This explains why the change in information technology, and the move to what I have called the "information-based organization" has made necessary massive "re-engineering."*

The new information technology underlies the strenuous efforts of American corporations in the last ten years to "re-engineer" themselves. Traditionally, most work in large American companies was organized on the baseball team model. Top management consisted of a chief executive officer to whom senior functional executives "reported," each doing a specific kind of work—running the factories, running sales, finance, and so on. The Office of the President is an attempt to convert top management into a doubles tennis team—made necessary (or, at least, possible) by the advent of information.

Traditionally, work on new products was done in a baseball-type team in which each function (design, engineering, manufacturing, marketing) did its own work, and then passed it on to the next. In some major American industries, for example, pharmaceuticals or chemicals, this was changed long ago into the soccer or symphony orchestra type of team. But the American automobile industry retained a baseball-type team structure for the design and introduction of new automobiles. Around 1970, the Japanese began to use information to switch to a soccer-type team for this work. As a result, Detroit fell way behind both in the speed with which it introduced new models and in its flexibility. Since 1980, Detroit has been trying desperately to catch up with the Japanese by changing the design and introduction of new automobiles to a soccer-type team. And on the factory floor the availability of information—which makes possible, in fact mandatory, the shift to "Total Quality Management"—is forcing Detroit to change from the baseball team, along which the traditional assembly line had been organized, to the doubles tennis team, which is the concept underlying "flexible manufacturing."

Only when the appropriate type of team has been chosen and established will work on the productivity of knowledge workers and service workers become truly effective. The right

* See *The New Realities*, Chapter 14.

team by itself does not guarantee productivity. But the wrong team destroys productivity.

THE NEED TO CONCENTRATE

Concentration on job and task is the last prerequisite for productivity in knowledge and service work. In the work on making and doing things, the task is clearly defined. The worker shoveling sand, whose task Taylor studied a century ago, was not expected to bring the sand to where he could begin shoveling it. That was somebody else's job. The farmer plowing the field does not climb off the tractor to attend a meeting. In machine-paced work, the machine concentrates the worker; the worker is servant to the machine. In knowledge work and in most service work, where the machine (if any) is a servant to the worker, productivity requires the elimination of whatever activities do not contribute to performance. They sidetrack and divert from performance. Eliminating such work may be the single biggest step toward greater productivity in both knowledge and service work.

> The task of nurses in hospitals is patient care. But every study shows that they spend up to three quarters of their time on work that does not contribute to patient care. Instead, two thirds or three quarters of the nurse's time is typically spent filling out papers. Whenever we analyze the performance of salespeople in the department store, we find that they spend more than half their time on work that does not contribute to their performance, that is, satisfying the customer. They spend at least half their time filling out papers that serve the computer rather than the customer. Whenever we analyze the time spent by engineers, we find that half their time is spent attending meetings or polishing reports which have very little to do with their own task. This not only destroys productivity; it also destroys motivation and pride.

Wherever a hospital concentrates paperwork and assigns it to a floor clerk who does nothing else, nurses' productivity doubles. So does their contentment. They then suddenly have time for the work they are trained and hired for: patient care. Similarly, both the productivity and satisfaction of salespeople in department stores shoot up overnight when the paperwork is taken out of their job and concentrated with a floor clerk. And the same happens when engineers are relieved of their "chores"—draftsman's work, rewriting reports and memos, or attending meetings.

Knowledge workers and service workers should always be asked: "Is this work necessary to your main task? Does it contribute to your performance? Does it help you do your own job?" And if the answer is no, the procedure or operation must be considered a "chore" rather than "work." It should either be dropped altogether or engineered into a job of its own.

Defining performance; determining the appropriate work flow; setting up the right team; and concentrating on work and achievement are prerequisites for productivity in knowledge work and service work. Only when they have been done can we begin the work on making productive the individual job and the individual task.

Frederick Winslow Taylor is usually criticized for not asking the workers how to do the job. He told them. But so did George Elton Mayo (1880–1949), the Australian-born Harvard psychologist who in the 1920s and 1930s attempted to replace Taylor's "Scientific Management" with "Human Relations." Lenin and Stalin did not consult the "masses," either; they told them. Freud never asked patients what they thought their problem might be. And only toward the end of World War II did it occur to any high command to consult the users—the soldiers in the field—before introducing a new weapon. The nineteenth century believed in the expert knowing the answers.

By now we have learned that those who actually do a job know more about it than anybody else. They may not know how to interpret their knowledge, but they do know what works and what doesn't. And so, in the last forty years, we have learned that work on improving any job or task begins with the people who actually do the work. They must be asked: "What can we learn from you? What do you have to tell us about the job and how it should be done? What tools do you need? What information do you need?" Workers must be required to take responsibility for their own productivity, and to *exercise control* over it.

We were first taught this lesson by American production in World War II.* But, as is well known, the Japanese were the first ones to apply the idea (if only because a few Americans, especially W. Edwards Deming and Joseph Juran, taught it to them).

After World War II, however, the United States, Great Britain, and Continental Europe all went back to the traditional "productivity by command" approach—largely as a result of strong labor union opposition to anything that would give the worker a "managerial attitude," let alone "managerial responsibility." Only in the last ten years has American management rediscovered the lesson of its own performance in World War II.

In making and moving things, partnership with a responsible worker is the best way. But Taylor's telling them worked, too, and quite well. In knowledge and service work, partnership with the responsible worker is the *only* way to improve productivity. Nothing else works at all.

Productivity in knowledge work and service work demands that we build continuous learning into the job and into the organization. Knowledge demands continuous learning because it is constantly changing. But service work, even of the purely clerical kind, also demands continuous self-improvement, continuous learning. The best way for people to learn how to be more productive is for them to teach. To obtain the improvement in productivity which the post-capitalist society now needs, the organization has to become both a learning and a teaching organization.

---

* My two books *The Future of Industrial Man* (1942) and *The New Society* (1949), were the first to draw this conclusion from the World War II experience. In them, I argued for the "responsible worker" taking "managerial responsibility." As a result of their wartime experiences, W. Edwards Deming and Joseph Juran each developed what we now call "Quality Circles" and "Total Quality Management." Finally, the idea was forcefully presented by Douglas McGregor in his well-known book *The Human Side of Enterprise* (New York: McGraw-Hill, 1960), with his "Theory X" and "Theory Y."

RESTRUCTURING ORGANIZATIONS

Improving the productivity of knowledge workers and service workers will demand fundamental changes in the structure of organizations. It may even require *totally new organizations.*

Re-engineering the team so that work can flow properly will lead to the elimination of most "management layers." In the symphony orchestra, several hundred highly skilled musicians play together; but there is only one "executive," the conductor, with no intermediate layers between him (or her) and the orchestra members. This will be the organization model for the new, information-based organization. We will thus see a radical shift from the tradition in which performance was primarily rewarded by advancement into command positions, that is, into managerial ranks. Organizations will have very few such command positions. We will increasingly see organizations operating like the jazz combo, in which leadership within the team shifts with the specific assignment and is independent of the "rank" of each member. In fact, the word "rank" should disappear totally from the vocabulary of knowledge work and knowledge worker. It should be replaced by "assignment."

This shift will raise tremendous problems of motivation, of reward, and of recognition.

THE CASE FOR OUTSOURCING

Even more drastic, indeed revolutionary, are the requirements for obtaining productivity from service workers. Service work in many cases will be contracted out of the organization to whom the service is being rendered. This applies particularly to support work, such as maintenance, and to a good deal of clerical work. "Outsourcing," moreover, will be applied increasingly to such work as drafting for architects and to the technical or professional library. In fact, American law firms already contract out to an outside computerized "database" most of what their own law library used to do.

One driving force behind outsourcing is the need to make service workers productive. The greatest need for increased productivity is in activities which do not lead to promotion into senior management within the organization. But nobody in senior management is likely to be much interested in this kind of work, know enough about it, care greatly for it, or even consider it important—no matter how much money is at stake. Such work does not fit the organization's value system.

In the hospital, for instance, the value system is that of the doctors and nurses. They are concerned with patient care. No one therefore pays much attention to maintenance work, support work, clerical work—even though that is where half the hospital's costs are likely to be. Nobody from these support activities can expect ever to get into a senior hospital position.

> Most of the women who start cleaning hospital floors or making hospital beds, fifteen years later will still be cleaning hospital floors or making hospital beds. By contrast, the woman who as a senior vice president heads the hospital division of America's largest maintenance company started as an almost illiterate Mexican immigrant with a pail and a broom fourteen years ago. But she started working in a hospital where maintenance work had been contracted out to a maintenance company. As a result, she had opportunities for advancement. Productivity in the hospitals maintained by this company has almost tripled in the last fifteen years. The time needed to make a bed, for instance, has been cut by two thirds.

This maintenance company had a financial interest in improving the productivity of its menial jobs. It had people in executive positions who knew firsthand the work needed to maintain a hospital. The company was therefore willing to work for years on the redesign of all the tools needed, right down to the bed sheets. It was willing to invest substantial capital in the new methods. None of this a hospital would have done. To make hospital maintenance productive required an outside contractor.

The greatest need for outsourcing—whether of manual work like maintenance, or clerical work like billing—is found in government (see Chapter 8 below). There, productivity is lowest. There, also, are the most people employed in such support activities.

But large businesses are not much different. They, too, require systematic contracting out of service work to organizations whose business it is to do such work. These contracting organizations offer career opportunities for the people doing such work. Their executives take such work seriously; they are therefore willing to invest time and money in redesigning the work and its tools. They are willing, even eager, to do the hard work needed to improve productivity. Above all, they take the people who do such work seriously enough to challenge them to take the lead in improving their work and its productivity.

Outsourcing is necessary not just because of the economics involved. It is necessary because it provides opportunities, income, and dignity for service workers.

We should therefore expect within a fairly short period of years to find such work contracted out to independent organizations, which compete and get paid for their own effectiveness in making this kind of work more productive.

This means a radical change in structure for the organizations of tomorrow. It means that the big business, the government agency, the large hospital, the large university will not necessarily be the one that employs a great many people. It *will* be the one that has substantial revenues and substantial results—achieved in large part because it itself does only work that is focused on its mission; work that is directly related to its results; work that it recognizes, values, and rewards appropriately. The rest it contracts out.

AVERTING A NEW CLASS CONFLICT

The rapid increase in productivity of the workers making and moving things overcame the nineteenth century's nightmare of "class conflict." Now, a rapid increase in the productivity of service workers is required to avert the danger of a new "class conflict" between the two new dominant groups in the post-capitalist society: knowledge workers and service workers. To make service work productive is thus the first social priority of the post-capitalist society, in addition to being an economic priority.

Knowledge workers and service workers are not "classes" in the traditional sense. The line between the two is porous. In the same family, there are likely to be service workers and knowledge workers who have advanced education. But there is a danger that the post-capitalist society will become a class society unless service workers attain both income and dignity. This requires productivity. But it also requires opportunities for advancement and recognition.

The structure of the post-capitalist society will therefore be different from either the earlier capitalist or the socialist society. There, organizations tried to encompass the maximum of activities. Organizations of the post-capitalist society, by contrast, will concentrate on their core tasks. For the rest, they will work with other organizations in a bewildering variety of alliances and partnerships. Both capitalist and socialist societies were, to use a scientific metaphor, "crystalline" in their structure. Post-capitalist society is more likely to resemble a liquid.

5

The Responsibility-Based Organization

POLITICAL AND SOCIAL THEORY, since Plato and Aristotle, has focused on power. But responsibility must be the principle which informs and organizes the post-capitalist society. The society of organizations, the knowledge society, demands *a responsibility-based organization.*

Organizations must take responsibility for the limit of their power, that is, for the point at which exercising their function ceases to be legitimate.

Organizations have to take "social responsibility." There is no one else around in the society of organizations to take care of society itself. Yet they must do so responsibly, within the limits of their competence, and without endangering their performance capacity.

Organizations, in order to function, have to have considerable power. What is legitimate power? What are its limits? What should they be?

Finally, organizations themselves must be built on *responsibility from within,* rather than on power or on command and control.

WHERE RIGHT BECOMES WRONG

In the 1930s, John L. Lewis (1880–1969) was considered the second most powerful man in America after President Franklin D. Roosevelt. In fact, Roosevelt owed his election in large part to Lewis, who, until then a lifelong Republican, led his coal miners' union, the United Mine Workers of America (UMW), and with it the entire American labor movement, into the Democratic camp at the 1932 convention. He then led the unionization drive of the New Deal years and became the head of a new and powerful labor organization, the Congress of Industrial Organizations.

But in 1943 Lewis rebelled against the wage freeze imposed during World War II and pulled his coal miners out on strike. President Roosevelt appealed to him to heed the national interest and call off the strike. But Lewis refused. "The President of the United States," he said, "is paid to look after the national interest. I am paid to look after the interests of the miners."

War production was just starting up. American soldiers were already in combat, both in Europe and in the Pacific, but they still woefully lacked equipment and ammunition, and were suffering heavy casualties because of these shortages. The entire war effort was fueled by coal, and the country could not afford to lose even one day's coal production. Furthermore, the miners were the highest paid workers in America; compared to the pay of the men in uniform, they were plutocrats.

But Lewis won the strike.

He immediately lost, however, all power, all influence, all respect—even within the labor movement, and indeed even within his own union. The UMW itself immediately began to decline in power, influence, and membership. Ten years later, coal strikes had become non-events. In fact, Lewis's Pyrrhic victory in 1943 marked the beginning of the decline of unionism in the United States.

Lewis lived long enough to see the consequences of his "victory." But he maintained to his dying day that he was right in calling the strike, that it was his duty to do so. "What is good for labor," he repeatedly said, "is ultimately good for the country. And a war is the only time when labor is needed, the only time when it has any real power, the only time when its legitimate claims for decent pay can be successfully pressed." He could never, it is reported, understand why the American public did not agree.

This is, of course, an extreme case. But it is also a revealing one. Lewis *knew* that he was in the right. But at what point does the right of an organization turn into social wrong; at what point is its function no longer legitimate?

These days there is a great deal of concern in the United States about "business ethics." But most of the discussion—and the courses under this title taught in business schools—deals with wrongdoing, for example, giving bribes or covering up for defective or harmful products. That wrongdoers in high places always plead their allegiance to a "higher good" is nothing new. All that needs to be said on the subject was said some three centuries ago by the great seventeenth-century French mathematician-philosopher Blaise Pascal in his *Letters to a Provincial* (1656–57), which demolished once and for all the Jesuit ethics of casuistry, the plea for a special ethics of power.

But the Lewis story does not deal with "wrong against wrong." It deals with "right against right." While not totally unprecedented, this is a new problem. It may be considered the central problem of responsibility within the society of organizations.

To be able to perform, an organization and its people must believe—as John L. Lewis did—that its own specialized task is the most important task in society. As we saw earlier, hospitals must believe that nothing matters as much as curing the sick. Businesses must believe that nothing matters as much as satisfying the material wants and needs of the community; and, in particular, that no product or service is nearly as vital to economy and community as the product or service "our business" produces and delivers. Labor unions must believe that nothing matters except the rights of the laboring man. Churches must believe that nothing matters except faith. Schools must believe that education is the one absolute good. And so on.

These organizations must be self-centered. Collectively, they discharge the tasks of society. But each discharges only one task, sees only one task.

In fact, we expect the leaders of these organizations to believe, as Lewis did, that their organization is *the* organization, that it *is* society.

> During his lifetime, Charles E. Wilson (1890–1961) was a prominent personality on the American scene, first as president and CEO of General Motors, the world's largest and most successful manufacturer at that time, and then, from 1953 to 1957, as Secretary of Defense in the Eisenhower administration. If he is remembered at all today, however, it is for something he did *not* say: "What is good for General Motors is good for the United States." What Wilson did say in his 1953 confirmation hearings for the Defense Department job was: "What is good for the United States is good for GM." Wilson tried all the remaining years of his life to correct the misquote, but no one listened to him. Everyone argued: "If he didn't say it, he surely believes it—in fact, he should believe it."

Where, then, are the limits? In an emergency such as a war or a great natural catastrophe, the answer is fairly simple: The survival of society comes before the survival of any one of its organs. But outside of such crises, there are no hard and fast answers. The only way to approach the problem is as the joint responsibility of the leaders of our organizations.

The closest approach so far is probably that of Japanese big business in the post–World War II period. In their planning during those years, business leaders started out with the question: "What is best for Japan, its society, its economy?" They then asked: "How can we turn this into an opportunity for business in general, and for our business in particular?" They were not "altruistic" or "selfless"; on the contrary, they were extremely profit-conscious. They did not "take leadership"; they accepted responsibility. But even in Japan, business and its leaders became self-centered again once their country fully emerged from post-war reconstruction and into economic world leadership.

WHAT IS SOCIAL RESPONSIBILITY?

The organizations of the society of organizations are special-purpose organs. Each is good at only one task; and this special-ization alone gives them their capacity to perform.

Organizations can only do damage to themselves and to society if they tackle tasks that are beyond their specialized com-petence, their specialized values, their specialized functions. The American hospital did a good deal of harm to itself and little good to the community when it attempted to take on the inner city's social ills by founding "inner-city clinics." The American school has failed miserably to produce racial integration. In both cases, the causes are undoubtedly good; they cry out for action. But the action needed—or at least the action chosen by these various organizations—was beyond such organizations' focus and function, and totally beyond their competence.

And yet who else is there to take care of society, its problems and its ills? These organizations collectively *are* society. It is futile to argue, as does the American economist and Nobel laureate Milton Friedman (b. 1912), that a business has only one respon-sibility: economic performance. Economic performance is the *first* responsibility of a business. A business that does not show a profit at least equal to its cost of capital is socially irresponsible. It wastes society's resources. Economic performance is the basis; without it, a business cannot discharge any other responsibilities, cannot be a good employer, a good citizen, a good neighbor.

But economic performance is not the sole responsibility of a business. Nor is educational performance the sole responsibility of a school or health-care performance the sole responsibility of a hospital. Power must always be balanced by responsibility; other-wise it becomes tyranny. Without responsibility, power also always degenerates into non-performance. And organizations *do* have power, albeit only social power.

The demand for the social responsibility of organizations will not go away. Hitherto we have talked mainly of the social responsibility of business, for a simple reason: business was the first of the new organizations to emerge. Increasingly, we will concern ourselves with the social responsibilities of other organizations, above all, with that of the university, which has a social monopoly—a power no other institution ever held before.

We do know, if only in rough outline, what the answer to the social responsibility problem has to be. An organization has full responsibility for its impact on community and society, for the effluents it discharges into a local river, for example, or the traffic jam its work schedules create on the city streets. It is, however, irresponsible for an organization to accept, let alone to pursue, responsibilities that would seriously impede its capacity to perform its main task and mission. And where it has no competence, it has no responsibility.

But—and it is a big "but"—organizations do have a responsibility to find an approach to basic social problems that can match their competence and can, in fact, render social problems an opportunity for the organization.

POWER AND ORGANIZATIONS

There is a further limit to the social action of organizations within the society of organizations: They are social institutions. They have neither legitimacy nor competence in politics.

The organizations of post-capitalist society all want things from the political power, the government. But they want things that are of benefit to them, that will enable them (at least in their opinion) better to do their own job, fit into their value system, or line their pockets. They are not and should not be concerned with political power for themselves. They are concerned with *function*.

This is in striking contrast to all earlier pluralist societies. They all were pluralisms of competing power centers. The pluralism of the society of organizations is one of discrete organizations, operating in tandem rather than in competition. The business enterprise does not compete with the hospital for patients or for the patronage of physicians; and the hospital in turn does not try to sell computers in competition with IBM. Each is the other's supplier and customer. The barons, counts, dukes, and bishops of medieval Europe and the *daimyos* of medieval Japan constantly waged war on each other. Modern organizations *lobby*.

In fact, nothing is as damaging to an organization as an attempt at political power. It always ends in disaster. In Argentina, Brazil, and Peru, the army was the most highly respected institution in each country until it seized power during the 1960s and 1970s. In each case, the military took action only because the country was on the point of total collapse. In each case, it came into power with substantial, perhaps even overwhelming, popular support. But in each case, when it relinquished power, it had become corrupted, discredited, demoralized, and almost destroyed.

In twentieth-century demonology, a popular figure has been the sinister business executive plotting for political power. But no successful business executive was ever greatly interested in power; they were interested in products, markets, revenues.

Businessmen who try to enter politics after a successful business career are not uncommon—though rarely successful. But I know of only two businessmen, both German—Hugo Stinnes (1870–1924) and Alfred Hugenberg (1865–1951)—who tried to use their business positions to dominate government and politics, Stinnes in the early 1920s, Hugenberg a few years later. Both did immeasurable damage to the Weimar Republic, and were largely responsible for Hitler's eventual triumph. But both failed politically; and the attempt at political power in the end destroyed their businesses and the men themselves.

Even labor leaders destroy themselves and their unions when they reach for political powers.

In the early 1970s, the British Coal Miners Union leader Arthur Scargill seemed England's most powerful man. Then, in

1974, he called a strike to break the Tory government and establish himself as the country's most powerful politician. Just as John L. Lewis had done thirty years earlier in the United States, he won the strike; the government actually fell. But Scargill was finished, and so was his union. Ten years later, he again called a strike to re-establish his power and defeat another Conservative prime minister. Margaret Thatcher broke the strike with overwhelming public support, which even included a good many of Scargill's own miners. All Scargill accomplished was to enable Mrs. Thatcher to enact legislation sharply curtailing the power of unions and union leaders.

Yet the labor union remains the most nearly political of all the major organizations of the society of organizations. It has to be. It cannot exist, let alone prosper, unless government supports it. Very few, if any, union gains in developed countries have been attained by union action alone; most have been attained through legislation. But even unions succeed only if they use their strength to further the "cause of the laboring man," that is, to carry out their *proper function*.

Still, the organization has social power, and a good deal of it. It needs power to make decisions about people—whom to hire, whom to fire, whom to promote. It needs power to establish the rules and the discipline needed to produce results—for example, assignment of jobs and tasks to individuals, and establishment of working hours. It needs power to decide which factories to build and where, and which factories to close. It needs power to set prices.

Non-business organizations actually wield the greatest social power. Few organizations in history have been granted the amount of power that today's university has. Refusal to admit or to grant the diploma is tantamount to debarring a person from access to a career. Similarly, the power of the American hospital to deny a physician hospital privileges virtually excludes that physician from practicing medicine. A labor union's power to deny admission to apprenticeship, or its control of access to employment in a closed shop where only union members can be hired, equally gives the union tremendous social power.

This power can be regulated, limited, and restrained by the political power. It can be made subject to due process and to review by the law courts. But the social power of organizations cannot be exercised by the political authorities. It must be exercised by the individual organization.

The first answer to this problem is that no organization must be allowed power unless it is absolutely necessary to the discharge of its function. Anything beyond this must be viewed as usurpation.

A second answer is that the exercise of the organization's legitimate power must be safeguarded against the abuse of power. There must be clear and public rules for its exercise, and there must be review and appeal to some person or some tribunal that is impartial and not part of the problem. There must be what lawyers call "due process."

> The bishop has far more power over the priests of his Catholic Diocese than most chief executive officers of other organizations. But he cannot remove a priest from his parish or fire him. This can be done only by the Diocesan Court, and only "for cause." And while the bishop appoints the members of the court, he cannot remove them during their fixed term of office.

But the most important answer to the problem of the power of the organization is conversion from a power-based to a responsibility-based organization. It is the only answer, moreover, that fits the knowledge organization.

When modern organizations first arose one hundred and thirty years ago, they were modeled after the first, and at that time the most successful, of the new organizations: the army as it had been restructured in Prussia between 1855 and 1865. That army was, of necessity, based on command and control. A very small number of highly trained people at the top commanded a very large number of unskilled people drilled in a few repetitive motions. The Prussian Army which won such easy victories over Austria and France—both nations fielding larger forces and the second one also better armed—was, in effect, an "assembly line," and a highly efficient one. Such knowledge as it needed was provided by special "staffs" (i.e., the renowned Prussian General Staff), which were separate from the "line," that is, from doing.

This organization structure reached its peak in the late 1920s. Those years saw both its extension into all kinds of non-military work, and the development of more and more specialized staffs.

World War II was won by the United States in large part because the United States had been most successful in projecting a command and control organization into the economic sphere, industrial production and logistics. But by World War II it had also become clear that the command and control organization was rapidly growing outdated and was no longer adequate to the needs of the future. It was also becoming clear that the much-publicized attempt of those years to modify the command and control model by giving the worker a "feeling" of responsibility—the essence of the Harvard-based "Human Relations" School—was not going to succeed. Far more was needed than mere psychological manipulation.

> In those years, I first began to talk of the "responsible worker" who would have a "managerial attitude" and take "managerial responsibility." But only in Japan did industry pay heed, and even there only to a limited extent. It was actually in the military that the transformation of organization first began. To this day, the military, especially in the United States, has gone furthest in changing the structure of its organization from one based on command and control to one based on responsibility.

FROM COMMAND TO INFORMATION

By 1970, information had begun to transform organizations. We soon learned that the introduction into organization of information as a structural and organic element means the elimination of many, if not most, layers of management. In the traditional organization, most of the people called "managers" do not actually manage; they relay orders downward and information upward. When information becomes available, they become redundant.

But today we have to go beyond the information-based organization to the responsibility-based organization. And in knowledge work, as we have seen, the organization is increasingly composed of specialists, each of whom knows more about his or her own specialty than anybody else in the organization. The old-type organization assumed that the superior knew what the subordinate was doing—for the superior, only a few years earlier, had occupied the subordinate's position. The knowledge-based organization, by contrast, has to assume that superiors do not know the job of their subordinates. They have never held it.

Conductors do not know how the oboe does its work, but they know what the oboe should contribute. The surgeon similarly knows what the anesthesiologist should contribute, even though he or she cannot tell the anesthesiologist how to do the job. Both conductor and surgeon can still appraise the performance of their teammates. But in knowledge-based organizations, there is frequently no one who knows enough about the work of the specialist to appraise what that specialist actually contributes. Marketing people are not knowledgeable enough to appraise the performance of market researchers; they do not even understand the researchers' language or their statistical techniques.

Sales managers are also unlikely ever to have done any sales forecasting or any pricing; they do not know enough to tell forecasters and pricers what to do. Similarly, hospital administrators have never done clinical testing and cannot tell the pathologist in the medical lab what good testing is or how it should be done. In today's military, the commanding officer of an air squadron cannot tell his crew chief what good maintenance means, let alone how to do it. Even on the factory floor (especially in highly automated production), workers increasingly have more knowledge of their jobs than their supervisor.

FROM INFORMATION TO RESPONSIBILITY

The knowledge-based organization therefore requires that everyone take responsibility for that organization's objectives, contribution, and, indeed, for its behavior as well.

This implies that all members of the organization must think through their objectives and their contributions, and then take responsibility for both. It implies that there are no "subordinates"; there are only "associates." Furthermore, in the knowledge-based organization all members have to be able to control their own work by feedback from their results to their objectives.* All members must ask themselves: "What is the one *major* contribution to this organization and its mission which I can make at this particular time?" It requires, in other words, that all members act as responsible decision makers. All members have to see themselves as "executives."

Next it is the responsibility of all members to communicate their objectives, their priorities, and their intended contributions to their fellow workers—up, down, and sideways. And it is the responsibility of all members to make sure that their own objectives fit in with the objectives of the entire group.

This responsibility for thinking through what one's contribution should be and one's own responsibility as a knowledge worker, rests on each individual. In the knowledge organization it becomes everybody's responsibility, regardless of his or her particular job.

The ninety-seven technicians in a steelmaking minimill are legally "workers." But they control the machines which turn out as much steel as a conventional integrated steel mill does with a thousand people. Every one of these technicians constantly makes critical decisions at his or her computerized work station. They can be trained—they need to be trained. But they cannot be commanded. Each makes decisions all the time that have a greater impact on the

* What forty years ago, in *The Practice of Management* (1954), I called "Management by Objectives and *Self-Control*."

results of the minimill than even middle managers ever had in the conventional steel mill. Each of them has to be asked, "What should we hold *you* accountable for?" "What information do *you* need"? and, in turn, "What information do *you* owe the rest of us?" This means that each worker has to be a participant in decisions as to what equipment is needed; how the work should be scheduled; indeed, what the basic business policy of the entire mill should be. In the minimill, the entire group is a team in which each member has responsibility for the performance of the organization.

Even organizations which at first glance do only low-skilled or unskilled work need to be restructured as responsibility-based organizations. A small number of companies—one in Denmark, one in the United States, one in Japan—have been successful in greatly increasing the productivity of people who do unskilled, indeed menial, work, such as maintenance workers in hospitals, factories, or office buildings. They have achieved these increases by demanding responsibility from the very lowliest of their employees, those who start with a pail and a broom to clean floors, or those who clean offices after hours—for objectives, for contribution, for the performance of the entire team. These people know more about their jobs than anybody else. And when they are held responsible, they act responsibly.

TO MAKE EVERYBODY A CONTRIBUTOR

There is a great deal of talk today about "entitlement" and "empowerment." These terms express the demise of the command and control–based organization. But they are just as much terms of power and rank as the old terms were. We should instead be talking about responsibility and contribution. For power without responsibility is not power at all; it is irresponsibility.

Our aim should be to make people be more responsible. What we ought to be asking is not, "What should you be entitled to?" but, "What should you be responsible for?" The task of management in the knowledge-based organization is not to make everybody a boss. It is to make everybody a *contributor*.

PART TWO

POLITY

6

From Nation-State
to Megastate

I N POST-CAPITALIST SOCIETY, the changes in political structure
and polity (to use the old but perfect term for political society
and political system) are fully as great as the changes in society
and social structure. They are worldwide. And they are fully as
much accomplished fact.

Yesterday's world order is going fast, while tomorrow's world
order has yet to emerge. We are not in fact facing the "new world
order" today's politicians so constantly invoke. Rather, we are
facing a *new world disorder*—no one can know for how long.

In political structure and polity, too, we are moving into a
"post" age, the age of the post-sovereign state. We already know
the new forces—and they are quite different from those that have
governed political structure and polity for the past four hundred
years. We know the new demands and can delineate some of
them, maybe most. We do not, however, know the answers, the
solutions, the new integrations. Even more than in society and
social structure, the players on the stage—politicians, diplomats,
civil servants, political scientists, and political writers—speak and
write in yesterday's terms. And, by and large, they act—indeed,

they have to act—on yesterday's assumptions and have to base themselves on yesterday's realities.

THE PARADOX OF THE NATION-STATE

Everybody knows—and every history book teaches—that the last four hundred years of world history were the centuries of the Western nation-state. And for once, what everybody knows is true; but it is a paradoxical truth.

For the great political thrusts in these four centuries were all attempts to transcend the nation-state and to replace it with a transnational political system, whether a colonial empire or a European (or Asian) superstate. These were the centuries in which the great colonial empires rose and fell: the Spanish and Portuguese empires emerging in the sixteenth and collapsing in the early nineteenth century; then, beginning in the seventeenth and continuing into the twentieth century, the English, Dutch, French, and Russian empires. As soon as a new major player emerged on the stage of world history during these four centuries, that player immediately set about transcending the nation-state and transforming it into an empire—Germany and Italy, barely unified, went in for colonial expansion between 1880 and World War I, with Italy trying again as late as the 1930s. Even the United States became a colonial power in the early twentieth century. And so did the one non-Western country to become a nation-state, Japan.

In Europe itself, the home of the nation-state, these four centuries were dominated by one attempt after another to establish a transnational superstate. Six times in this period, a European nation-state attempted to become the ruler of Europe and to transform the continent into a European superstate under its control and domination. The first such attempt was made by Spain, beginning in the middle of the sixteenth century, when Spain itself was just emerging as a unified nation out of a congeries of squabbling kingdoms, duchies, counties, and free cities, precariously held together in the person of the Prince. Spain did not give up the dream of being master of Europe until a hundred years later, when it had all but ruined itself economically and militarily. Almost immediately, France, first under Richelieu, then under Louis XIV, took off where Spain had ended—again, to give up seventy-five years later, financially and spiritually exhausted. This did not deter another French ruler, Napoleon, only seventy-five years later, from trying again and subjecting all of Europe to twenty years of war and turmoil in his bid to become the ruler of Europe and build a French-dominated European superstate. Then, in this century, came the two German wars for mastery of Europe; and, after Hitler's defeat, Stalin's attempt to create, by force of arms and by subversion, a Soviet-ruled Europe. And just as Japan had tried to build a Western-style colonial empire as soon as it had become a nation-state, it too followed the Western example and tried, in this century, to create a Japanese-ruled Asian superstate.

In fact, it was not the nation-state that begat the empires. The nation-state itself arose as a response to transnational drives. The Spanish Empire in the Americas produced so much gold and silver that Spain, under Philip II, Charles V's son and successor, could finance the first standing army since the Roman legions, the Spanish Infantry—arguably the first "modern" organization. Thus equipped, Spain launched the first campaign for the mastery of Europe, the first attempt to unify Europe under Spanish rule. Countering Spain's threat became the motivation and avowed aim of the inventor of the nation-state, the French lawyer-politician Jean Bodin, in his book *Six Livres de la République* (1576). It was the Spanish threat that made Bodin's nation-state the "progressive" cause throughout Europe. And it was only because the threat was so great and so real that Bodin's recommendations were accepted. In the late sixteenth century, Bodin's model of the nation-state looked like pure fantasy. What Bodin prescribed was a centrally controlled civil service, answerable only to the sovereign; central control of the military, and a standing army officered by professional soldiers appointed by and accountable to central government; central control of coinage, taxes, customs; a centrally appointed professional judiciary rather than courts staffed by local magnates. All of these recommendations were the opposite

of what had existed for a thousand years, that is, since the collapse
of the Roman Empire. All of them threatened powerfully entrenched "special interests": an autonomous Church and exempt
bishoprics and abbeys; local lords of all sizes, each with his own
armed retainers owing fealty only to him, and each with his own
jurisdiction and his own taxing powers; free cities and self-
governing trade guilds; and scores of others. But the Spanish bid
for mastery of Europe left no alternative: the choice was subjec-
tion to the national sovereign or conquest by a foreign sovereign.
From then on, practically every change in the political structure of
the European nation-state was caused—or at least triggered—by
similar attempts to gain the mastery of Europe and to replace the
nation-state with a superstate, dominated in turn by France, Germany, or Russia.

One might therefore expect political scientists to have studied the colonial empire and to have developed a political theory
for it. They have done neither. Instead, they have focused on the
political theory and institutions of the nation-state. One might
have expected historians similarly to have studied the European
superstates. But in every university the prestigious chairs of history are chairs of *national* history. The famous history books all
deal with the nation-state—whether England or France, the
United States or Spain, Germany, Italy, or Russia. Even in Great
Britain, ruler of the biggest and, for many years, the most successful colonial empire, the study and teaching of history still
centers on the nation-state.*

* The United States is practically alone in having produced a first-rate
historian concerned with empire rather than with nation-state, William H.
Prescott (1796–1859), in his histories of the Spanish conquests of Mexico and of
Peru. One modern French historian of the first rank, Fernand Braudel (1902–
1985), did not confine himself to studying the nation-state. His vision took in all
of Europe; indeed, the entire world. But he was an economic and social rather
than a political historian. The two greatest nineteenth-century German historians who established history as a "science"—Leopold von Ranke and Theodor
Mommsen—did not confine themselves to German history. One of Ranke's
main works, for instance, was a history of the popes. And Mommsen's great
work was the history of Rome. But even they ignored the thrust toward empire
in modern politics and treated bids for the mastery of Europe as part of
national history rather than events transcending the nation-state and attempts
to replace it with a transnational political structure.

One reason for this neglect of empire and superstate is that neither developed institutions. To be sure, the House of Lords in London was the ultimate court of appeal for all British possessions. But this was quite incidental to its sitting as the court of appeal for the British Isles. Similarly, the British Parliament was in theory the legislative body for all British possessions. But all its members were elected from the United Kingdom, that is, solely from the British Isles. Only in times of crisis was it concerned with anything but U.K. affairs. The king or queen reigned over the entire British Empire; yet no British monarch set foot in any British possession until after it had ceased to be a British possession, after the empire had disappeared (when the present queen, Elizabeth II, began to visit former empire countries). Yet Britain came closer to building an empire than any other country.

The colonial "empires" were not fiction, but they were not "empires." They were nation-states with colonial possessions. One need only compare them with the political structure from which they took their names: the empire of the Romans. The age of the colonial empires lasted almost exactly as long as the Roman Empire, four hundred years, which should have been more than enough time for the political, social, and economic integration of mother country and empire. But no such task was even attempted.

The three greatest Roman emperors after Augustus—Trajan (reigned 98–117 A.D.), Hadrian (reigned 117–138), and Diocletian (reigned 284–305)—were "colonials": Trajan and Hadrian were born and raised in Spain, Diocletian was born and raised in present-day Yugoslavia. They were not of Latin stock, the first two probably Berbers, Diocletian an Illyrian or a Slav. But can one imagine the American George Washington, the South African Jan Smuts, or the Indian Jawaharlal Nehru as British prime ministers? Yet surely they were the ablest and most prominent English-speaking and English-cultured political leaders of their times, respectively at the end of the eighteenth century, after World War I, and after Churchill's defeat following World War II.

The most enduring legacy of the Roman Empire, which still undergirds European law and jurisprudence—the codification of the laws (the *Codex juris civilis*)—was written in Latin. But it was compiled in Greek-speaking Constantinople, at the behest of a Greek-speaking emperor, Justinian (A.D. 483–565), by scholars not one of whom was himself a Roman, and at a time when the Latin-speaking west of the empire had already succumbed to the barbarians.

And for hundreds of years after Rome's fall, every educated person in the former empire, even the most devout of Christians, thought of himself as a Roman, educated himself in the Latin of Cicero, and yearned back to the "glory that was Rome"—to Augustus, Trajan, Hadrian.

There were a good many settlers in the American thirteen colonies who considered themselves Englishmen rather than Americans during the American War of Independence, the first breakup of one of the modern empires. But these American "Loyalists" were the exception. Few "colonials" in Mexico, Colombia, or Brazil mourned the passing of the Spanish and Portuguese empires. And even fewer "colonials" mourned the disappearance of the twentieth-century empires of the British, French, Dutch, and Japanese. The British Raj in India gave birth to a remarkably large and distinguished upper class of truly bicultural people, many of them educated at the best English universities and all of them steeped in English poetry, English law, and English constitutional philosophy and history. Yet not one of these men held fast to the empire or to the imperial connection. Not one tried to find a constitutional solution to preserve the cultural community of empire while establishing Indian political autonomy. Instead, they became the most dedicated, most uncompromising agitators for Indian independence and for a separate Indian national state.

Even more amazing is the lack of integration in the Russian Empire. Ukrainians, White Russians, Armenians, Georgians, Germans—people of every European stock (excepting only Jews and Catholic Poles)—had for centuries been treated as equals, in both the Russia of the tsars and the Soviet Union of the Communists. All they had to do was to learn Russian. A large number of tsarist generals and ministers were of German origin, such as Count Witte, the reform-minded prime minister of the last Tsar.

Stalin was a Georgian; and the last chief of staff of the Soviet Army was a Ukrainian. Yet, as the Soviet Empire dissolves, there is virtually no pro-empire sentiment, no pro-empire party, no pro-empire movement. Resistance has been entirely in the name of nationalism rather than in that of empire. Ethnic Russians, living in what was becoming a new national state in, for example, Moldova or Latvia, protested against being made Moldovans or Latvians and demanded independence of their own.

This inability of the colonial empires to become anything more than administrative abstractions, this inability to become political societies, is all the more paradoxical as each came into being so very easily—one is tempted to say "naturally." While the Roman Empire was established in bloody war after bloody war, the modern colonial empires were established with a minimum of fighting. To be sure, the British fought in India—but primarily against the French rather than against Indian rulers. They fought a bitter war against the Boers in South Africa. But otherwise the British Empire was established with very little violence, except for local skirmishes involving no more than a thousand or so British fighting men. The Indian Mutiny of 1857 was the sole major uprising against British rule in the one hundred fifty years between American independence and the secession of Ireland after World War I.

Similarly, the only prolonged resistance the Russians encountered against the extension of their empire was in the Caucasus—not in the Ukraine, not in the Baltic States (annexed in the eighteenth century), not in Central Asia. The battles the French had to fight to establish their empire in Southeast Asia and in Africa were mere skirmishes, involving fewer soldiers than France (or any other European country) committed to trivial and insignificant European border conflicts.

And yet, the moment a European power showed any sign of weakness, its empire collapsed; and it collapsed into nation-states. The same was true for Japan. Even the so-called White Dominions of the British Empire—Australia, Canada, New Zealand—proud though they are of their English heritage and cultural tradition, became nation-states the moment they ceased to be "colonies." No other form of political integration was available.

The modern empire lacked integrative power. The nation-state alone could integrate, could form a polity—a political society—could create citizenship.

In Europe, too, none of the would-be conquerors could integrate the superstate into a political structure. All they could do—from Philip II through Stalin—was subjugate by brute force. Yet three of the attempts to create a European superstate were accompanied by ideologies with powerful appeal: Napoleon's attempt by *Liberté, Fraternité, Egalité*, the ideology of the French Revolution; Hitler's attempt by the ideology of hatred, envy, and anti-Semitism (holding far more appeal than we like to admit, which in large part explains why there was appeasement rather than resistance to Hitler in every Continental country until he had conquered it); and Stalin by the ideology of Marxist Socialism which, for a hundred years, had the strongest and widest appeal since Christianity. Even the Japanese attempt to create a Pan-Asian superstate was based on a powerful ideology: anti-Westernism and anti-colonialism.

Yet all of these attempts floundered on their inability to convert the conquered territories into a political structure, the failure to build political institutions, the failure to create anything even remotely comparable to St. Paul's claim, "*Civis romanus sum* (I am a Roman citizen)." Paul was a Jew by religion and race, a Greek by culture and language; but his "I am a Roman citizen" was a higher claim, both an appeal to a higher law and an assertion of a political identity that superseded geography, race, or language.

All modern empires and all superstates have foundered because of their inability to transcend the nation-state, let alone to become its successor.

But while the nation-state thus was the sole political reality in the centuries of empires and superstates, it has transformed itself profoundly in the last hundred years. *It mutated into the Megastate.*

THE DIMENSIONS OF THE MEGASTATE

By 1870, the nation-state had triumphed everywhere; even Austria had become Austria-Hungary, a federation of two nation-states. And the nation-states of 1870 still looked and acted like the sovereign nation-state Bodin had invented three hundred years earlier.

But the nation-state of 1970, a century later, bore little resemblance to Bodin's state or, indeed, to the nation-state of 1870. It had mutated into the *Megastate*—the same species perhaps as its 1870 progenitor, but as different from it as the panther is from the pussycat.*

The national state was designed to be the guardian of civil society. The Megastate became its master. And in its extreme, totalitarian form, it replaced civil society completely. In totalitarianism, all society became political society.

The national state was designed to protect both the citizen's life and liberty and the citizen's property against arbitrary acts of the sovereign. The Megastate, even in its least extreme, Anglo-American form, considers a citizen's property to be held only at the discretion of the tax collector. As Joseph Schumpeter first pointed out in his essay *Der Steuerstaat* (*The Fiscal State*, 1918), the Megastate asserts that citizens hold only what the state, expressly or tacitly, allows them to keep.

Bodin's national state had as its first function the maintenance of civil society, especially in times of war. This is in effect what "defense" meant. The Megastate has increasingly blurred the distinction between peacetime and wartime. Instead of peace, there is "Cold War."

---

* The first person to understand this was not a political scientist or a politician, but a novelist. Franz Kafka's two novels, *The Trial* and *The Castle* (both published in 1926, after his death), are the most penetrating analyses of the Megastate, as they were the earliest.

THE NANNY STATE

The shift from the national state to the Megastate began in the last decades of the nineteenth century. The first small step toward the Megastate was Bismarck's invention in the 1880s of the Welfare State. Bismarck's goal was to combat the rapidly rising socialist tide. It was a response to the threat of class war. Government had previously been perceived exclusively as a political agency. Bismarck made government into a social agency. His own welfare measures—health insurance, insurance against industrial accidents, old-age pensions (followed thirty years later, after World War I, by the British invention of unemployment insurance)—were modest enough. But the principle was radical; and it is the principle that has had far greater effect than the individual actions taken in its name.

In the German health insurance system, all employed people and their families have to be insured against illness, but with free choice of insurance carrier (and most insurance agencies are non-governmental). Unemployment insurance as the British instituted it made the state the insurance carrier; but again the state acted purely as a fiscal agent. Social Security, which brought the Welfare State to the United States in 1935–36, was organized on the same principle. So were most of the other social measures of the New Deal, for example, farm subsidies, or payments for putting land into "the soil bank," thus ensuring both reductions in surplus production of farm crops and welfare payments to the farmers.

In the 1920s and 1930s, Communists, Fascists, and Nazis took over social institutions. But in the democracies, government still only insured or, at most, offered payments. By and large it still stayed out of doing actual social work or forcing citizens into proper social behavior.

This changed rapidly after World War II. From being a provider, the state now became a *manager*. The last of the traditional Welfare State measures—and arguably the most successful one—was the U.S. G.I. Bill of Rights, enacted right after World

War II. It gave every returning American veteran the means to attend a college and to acquire higher education. The government did not, however, attempt to dictate which college a veteran should attend. It did not attempt to run any college. It offered money if the veteran chose to go to college; the veteran then decided where to go and what to study. And no college had to accept any applicant.

The other major social program of the immediate postwar period, the British National Health Service, was the first one (outside of the totalitarian countries) to take government beyond the role of insurer or provider. But only in part. For standard medical care, government in the National Health Service is an insurance carrier: it reimburses the physician who takes care of a patient. But the physician does not become a government employee; nor is the patient in any way limited as to which physician he or she chooses. On the other hand, hospitals and hospital care under the National Health Service *were* taken over by government. The people working in hospitals became government employees; and government actually manages the hospitals. This was the first step toward a changed role for government in the social sphere. Government ceased to be the rule setter, the facilitator, the insurer, the disbursement agent. It became the doer and the manager.

By 1960, it had become accepted doctrine in all developed Western countries that government is the appropriate agent for *all* social problems and *all* social tasks. In fact, nongovernmental, private activity in the social sphere became suspect; so-called liberals considered it "reactionary" or "discriminatory." In the United States, government became the actual doer in the social sphere, especially in the attempt to change human behavior in a multi-racial society by government action or government order. So far, the United States is the only country (outside of totalitarian ones) where government has attempted to command changes in social values and individual behavior in order to stamp out discrimination by race, age, or gender.

THE MEGASTATE AS MASTER OF THE ECONOMY

By the late nineteenth century, the nation-state was being made over into an economic agency. The first steps were taken in the United States, which invented both governmental regulation of business and governmental ownership of the new businesses of a capitalist economy. Beginning in the 1870s, regulation of business—banking, railways, electric power, telephones—was gradually established in the United States. Such government regulation—one of the most original political inventions of the nineteenth century, and initially a hugely successful one—was clearly seen from the beginning as a "third way" between "unfettered" Capitalism and Socialism, and as a response to the tensions and problems created by the rapid spread of capitalism and technology.

A few years later, the United States began to take businesses into government ownership—first in the 1880s in the state of Nebraska under the leadership of William Jennings Bryan. Another few years later, between 1897–1900, Karl Lueger (1844–1910), mayor of Vienna, expropriated and took into municipal ownership the streetcar companies and the electric power and gas companies of the Austrian capital. Like Bismarck, who had acted to combat Socialism, neither Bryan nor Lueger were Socialists as such; both were what the United States calls "Populists." Both saw in government ownership primarily a means of assuaging a rapidly escalating class war between "capital" and "labor."

Still, few people in the nineteenth century—indeed, few people before 1929—believed that government could or should manage the economy, let alone that government could or should control recessions and depressions. Most economists believed that a market economy is "self-regulating." Even Socialists believed that the economy would regulate itself once private property had been abolished. The job of the nation-state and of its government was seen as maintaining the "climate" for economic growth and prosperity—by keeping the currency stable, taxes

124

low, and by encouraging thrift and savings. Economic "weather," i.e., economic fluctuations, was beyond anyone's control, if only because the events causing these fluctuations were likely to be world market events rather than events within the nation-state itself.

The Great Depression gave rise to the belief that the national government is—and should be—in control of the economic weather. The English economist John Maynard Keynes (1883–1946) first asserted that the national economy is insulated from the world economy, at least in mid-sized and large countries. Then he claimed that this insulated national economy is totally determined by governmental policy, to whit, by government spending. However much today's economists otherwise differ from Keynes, Friedmanites, supply-siders, and the other post-Keynesians all follow Keynes in these two tenets. They all consider the nation-state and its government the master of the national economy and the controller of its economic weather.

THE FISCAL STATE

The two world wars of this century transformed the nation-state into a "fiscal state."

Until World War I, no government in history was ever able—even in wartime—to obtain from its people more than a very small fraction of the country's national income, perhaps 5 or 6 percent. But in World War I every belligerent, even the poorest, found that there was practically no limit to what government can squeeze out of the population. By the outbreak of World War I, the economies of all the belligerent countries were fully monetized. As a result, the two poorest countries, Austria-Hungary and Russia, in several war years could actually tax and borrow more than the total annual income of their respective populations. They managed to liquidate capital accumulated over long decades and turn it into war materiel.

Joseph Schumpeter, who was then still living in Austria, understood immediately what had happened. But the rest of the economists and most governments needed a second lesson: World War II. Since then, however, all developed and many developing countries have become "fiscal states." They have all come to believe that there are no *economic* limits to what government can tax or borrow and, therefore, no economic limits to what government can spend.

What Schumpeter pointed out was that as long as governments have been around, the budget process has begun with an assessment of the available revenues. Expenditures then had to be fitted to these revenues. And since the supply of "good causes" is inexhaustible, and the demand for spending therefore infinite, the budgeting process mostly consisted of deciding where to say no. As long as revenues were known to be limited, governments, whether democracies or absolute monarchies like the Russian tsars, operated under extreme restraints. These restraints made it impossible for the government to act as either a social or an economic agency.

But since World War I—and even more noticeably since World War II—the budgeting process has meant, in effect, saying yes to everything.

Traditionally, government, the political society, had available to it only such means as were granted by the civil society, and then only within the very narrow limits of a few percentage points of national income, which was all that could be monetized. Only that amount could be converted into taxes and loans, and hence into government revenues. Under the new dispensation, which assumes that there are no economic limits to the revenues it can obtain, government becomes the master of civil society, able to mold and shape it. Above all, by using taxes and expenditures, government can redistribute society's income. Through the power of the purse, it can shape society in the politician's image.

But also under the new dispensation it is only too easy to see national income as belonging to government, with individuals entitled only to whatever government is willing to let them have. Before 1914—actually, before 1946—nobody spoke of "tax loopholes." The assumption in earlier days was that everything belonged to the individual, unless it had been expressly conveyed to government by the taxpayers' political representatives, whether an absolute government or a parliament.

The term "tax loophole," however, implies that everything belongs to government unless it has been specifically designated to be retained by the taxpayer. And whatever taxpayers retain, they retain only because government in its wisdom and generosity is willing to allow them to do so.

Of course, this became explicit only in the Communist countries. But even in the United States, especially during the Kennedy years, it was received wisdom in Washington, particularly among the bureaucracy, that all income belongs to government except whatever government expressly and explicitly permits the taxpayer to keep.

THE COLD WAR STATE

The Welfare State, government as the master of the economy, and the fiscal state each arose out of social and economic problems, and social and economic theories. The last of the mutations that created the Megastate, the Cold War State, was a response to technology.

Its origin was the German decision, in the 1890s, to build in peacetime a massive naval deterrent. This started the armaments race. The Germans knew that they were taking an enormous political risk; in fact, most politicians resisted the decision. But the German admirals were convinced that technology left them no choice. A modern navy meant steel-clad ships, and such ships had to be built in peacetime. To wait for the outbreak of war, as traditional policy dictated, would have meant waiting too long.

Since 1500 or so, when the knight had become obsolete, warfare increasingly was waged with weapons produced in ordinary peacetime facilities with the minimum of delay or adaptation. In the American Civil War, cannons were still being produced in hastily adapted peacetime workshops and factories after hostilities had broken out. Textile mills switched production practically overnight from civilian clothing to uniforms. Indeed, the two major wars fought during the second half of the nineteenth century, the American Civil War (1861–65) and the Franco-Prussian War (1870–71), were still largely fought by civilians who had put on their uniforms only a few weeks before engaging in combat.

Modern technology—the German admirals of 1890 argued—had changed all this. The wartime economy could no longer be an adaptation of the peacetime economy. The two had to be separate. Both weapons and fighting men had to be made available, in large quantities, *before* the outbreak of hostilities. To produce either required increasingly long lead times.

Defense, it was implicit in the German argument, no longer means keeping warfare away from civilian society and civilian economy. Under conditions of modern technology, defense means a permanent wartime society and a permanent wartime economy. It means the "Cold War State."

The most astute political observer around the turn of the century, the French Socialist leader Jean Jaurès (1859–1914), understood this even before World War I. President Woodrow Wilson (1856–1924) learned it from World War I; it underlay his proposal for a League of Nations, that is, for a permanent organization monitoring national armaments. The first attempt to use military buildups as a means for arms control was the abortive Washington Naval Armaments Conference of 1923.

But even after World War II, the United States for a few short years tried to revert to a "normal" peacetime state. It tried to disarm as fast as possible, and as completely as possible. The coming of the Cold War in the Truman and Eisenhower years changed all this. Since then, the Cold War State has been the dominant organization of international politics.

By 1960, the Megastate had become a political reality in developed countries in all its aspects: as social agency; as master of the economy; as fiscal state; and in most countries as Cold War State.

THE JAPANESE EXCEPTION

The one exception is Japan. Whatever the truth about "Japan Inc."—and there is little truth to what is commonly understood in the West by this term—the Japanese after World War II did not adopt the Cold War State. Their government did not try to become master of the economy. It did not try to become master of society. Rather, it rebuilt itself after its shattering defeat on what in effect were traditional nineteenth-century lines. Militarily, of course, Japan had no choice. But Japan instituted almost no social programs. The only exception was national health insurance, largely imposed on it by the victorious Americans during the occupation. In effect, Japan was the only developed country—until Mrs. Thatcher's Britain began to privatize industry in the 1980s—in which industries that had earlier become nationalized (such as the steel industry) were returned to private ownership.

Viewed through the lens of traditional political theory of the eighteenth and early nineteenth centuries, Japan is clearly a "statist" country. But it is statist in the way in which Germany or France in 1880 or 1890 were "statist" compared to Great Britain or the United States. It has a large civil service (though no larger proportionately than the civil services of the English-speaking countries). Government service enjoys tremendous prestige and respect, the way government service in 1890 Germany, 1890 Austria-Hungary, or 1890 France enjoyed such respect. Government in Japan works closely with big business—again, no different from the way government in Continental Europe worked with economic interests during the late nineteenth century, and in fact not too different from the way American government worked with business or the farm interest around the turn of the century.

If the Megastate is taken as the norm—if reality rather than theory is the basis for judging political systems—Japan since World War II has been the country in which government has played the most restricted and in fact the most restrained role. It is exceedingly powerful in traditional nineteenth-century terms. It is least prominent in the spheres into which twentieth-century government has moved in the rest of the world. Government in Japan still functions primarily as a guardian.*

But except for Japan, the movement toward the Megastate has been universal throughout the developed world; and the developing countries rapidly followed suit. No sooner was a new nation-state formed out of the dissolution of an empire than it adopted the new military policy, building in peacetime a wartime military establishment, and manufacturing or at least procuring the advanced arms needed in case of war. It immediately attempted to get control of society. It immediately tried to use the tax mechanism to redistribute income. And finally, almost without exception, it tried to become the manager and, in large part, the owner of the economy.

In terms of political, intellectual, and religious freedom, the totalitarian countries (especially the Stalinist ones) and the democracies (which for a good many years meant primarily the English-speaking countries) were total antitheses. But in terms of the underlying theory of government, these systems differed more in degree than they did in kind. The democracies differed in how to do things; they differed far less in respect to *what* things should be done. They all saw government as the master of society and the master of the economy. And they all defined peace as equating with "Cold War."

HAS THE MEGASTATE WORKED?

Has the Megastate worked? In its most extreme manifestation, totalitarianism, whether of the Nazi or the Communist variety,

* In 1915, the brilliant American sociologist Thorstein Veblen in a book entitled *Imperial Germany and the Industrial Revolution* tried to explain the rise of Germany to economic dominance. Two thirds of a century later, an American economist, Chalmers Johnson, one of America's leading experts on Japanese economic policy, tried similarly to explain the rise of Japan to economic great power status in a book entitled *Miti and the Japanese Miracle* (Stanford University Press, 1982). Johnson clearly believes Japanese economic policies in the post–World War II period to be of purely Japanese origin and invention. Yet the resemblance to the policies Veblen described as the reasons for Germany's almost explosive economic growth in the forty years before World War I bear an uncanny resemblance to those Johnson describes.

has surely been a total failure—without a single redeeming feature. It may be argued that the Cold War State worked militarily for the USSR. For forty years, it was a military superpower. But the economic and social burden of the military establishment was so great as to become unbearable. It certainly contributed, and heavily, to the collapse of Communism and of the entire Soviet Empire.

But has the Megastate worked in its much more moderate form? Has it worked in the developed countries of Western Europe and in the United States? The answer is: Hardly any better. By and large it has been almost as great a fiasco there as in Hitler's Germany or in Stalin's Soviet Union.

The Megastate has been least successful as fiscal state. Nowhere has it succeeded in bringing about a meaningful redistribution of income. In fact, the past forty years have amply confirmed Pareto's Law, according to which income distribution between major classes in society is determined by two factors, and two factors only: the culture of the society, and the level of productivity within the economy. The more productive an economy, the greater the equality of income; the less productive, the greater the inequality of income. Taxes, so Pareto's Law asserts, cannot change this. But the advocates of the fiscal state based their case in large measure on the assertion that taxation could effectively and permanently change income distribution. All our experience of the last forty years disproves this claim.

The clearest case is the Soviet Union. Officially dedicated to equality, it established a very large *nomenklatura* of privileged functionaries who enjoyed income levels way beyond anything even the rich enjoyed under the tsars. The more Soviet productivity stagnated, the greater income inequality became in the Soviet Union. But the United States is also a good example. As long as American productivity increased, until the late 1960s or early 1970s, equality of income distribution increased steadily. While the rich were still getting richer, the poor were getting richer much faster, and the middle class got richer faster still. As soon as the productivity increases dropped or disappeared— that is, beginning with the Vietnam War—income inequality began to increase steadily, regardless of taxation. It made little difference that in the Nixon and Carter years the rich were taxed heavily or that in the Reagan years they were taxed much more lightly. Similarly, in the United Kingdom, despite a professed commitment to egalitarianism and a tax system designed to minimize income inequality, income distribution has become steadily less equal in the last thirty years as productivity stopped growing.

Despite all its corruptions and scandals, the most egalitarian country is now Japan—the country of the fastest productivity increases and the fewest attempts to redistribute income through taxation.

The other economic claim of the Megastate and of modern economic theory, that the economy can be successfully managed if government controls substantial parts of the gross national income, has equally been disproven. The Anglo-American countries fully embraced this theory. Yet there has been no decline in the number, the severity, or the length of their recessions. Recessions have been as numerous and have lasted just as long as they did in the nineteenth century. In the countries that did not embrace modern economic theory (Japan and Germany), recessions have been less frequent, less severe, and of shorter duration than in the countries that believe that the size of the government surplus or the government deficit (i.e., government spending) effectively manages the economy and can as effectively smooth out cyclical fluctuations.*

The sole result of the fiscal state has been the opposite of what it aims at: governments in all developed countries—and in most developing ones as well—have become such heavy spenders

* The one example always cited in support of modern economic theory and its claim to be able to control recessions, the so-called Kennedy tax cut of the early 1960s in the United States, is a mirage. There was no such tax cut. Federal taxes were indeed cut. But at the same time state and local governments increased their taxes beyond what the federal government cut, so that the total tax burden actually increased. Despite these moves, the economy recovered, precisely according to the timetable on which it would have recovered without government intervention.

that they cannot increase their expenditures in a recession. But that, of course, is the time when, according to economic theory, they should do so in order to create purchasing power and thus revive the economy. In every single developed country, governments have reached the limits of their ability to tax and their ability to borrow. They have reached these limits during boom times when, according to modern economic theory, they should have built up sizable surpluses. The fiscal state has spent itself into impotence.

Another basic tenet of the fiscal state has also been shown to be invalid. Central to Keynesian and post-Keynesian economic theory is the belief that the total tax take is the one thing that matters. The last forty years have proved that *what* is being taxed matters as much as *how much* is being taxed. What economists call the *incidence of taxation* is decisive—a notion that is dismissed rather contemptuously by post–World War II economists (see Chapter 8 below).*

THE PORK-BARREL STATE

Worst of all, the fiscal state has become a "pork-barrel state." If budget making starts with expenditures, there is no fiscal discipline; government spending becomes the means for politicians to buy votes. The strongest argument against the *ancien régime*, the eighteenth-century absolute monarchy, was that the king used the public purse to enrich his favorite courtiers. Fiscal accountability, and especially budget accountability to an elected legislature, was established to build accountability into government and to prevent courtiers from looting the commonwealth. In the fiscal state, the looting is done by politicians to ensure their own election.

An ever larger share of U.S. budgets—federal, state, munici-

* The basic work on this was done long before World War I by the American economist Edward R. A. Seligman (1861–1939), especially in his 1892 classic, *Shifting and Incidence of Taxation*.

pal—is spent on subsidies for very small groups of local constituents: a handful of tobacco farmers in North Carolina; an even smaller number of peanut growers in Georgia; sugarcane growers in Louisiana; obsolescent industries in a midwestern state; the wealthiest 5 percent of retired Social Security recipients; the owners of land taken over for a canal or a dam that serves no economic purpose; or the small town next to an army base that has no military significance. What actual proportion of total government spending in the United States goes to favors for constituents which serve no public policy purpose—and which in many cases are totally at odds with public policy—nobody quite knows. But it is very high in both federal and state budgets—far higher than most people realize. And in Japan, the extent to which a politician's role is seen increasingly as diverting large sums from the public purse to small numbers of constituents has become a public scandal.

But the most brazen and gigantic example of pork-barrel vote-buying occurred in Germany in the fall of 1990, when Chancellor Helmut Kohl saddled his country with the biggest peacetime public debt ever taken on in order to buy—successfully—the votes of his new constituents in the former East Germany. That was extremely popular at the time. Only two years later in the fall of 1992, it triggered the most severe financial and currency crisis in Europe since the Great Depression.

Democratic government rests on the belief that the first job of elected representatives is to defend their constituents against rapacious government. The pork-barrel state thus increasingly undermines the foundations of a free society. The elected representatives fleece their constituents to enrich special-interest groups and thereby to buy their votes. This is a denial of the concept of citizenship—and is beginning to be seen as such. The fact that it is undermining the very foundations of representative government is shown by the steady decline in voting participation. It is shown also by the steady decline in all countries of interest in the function of government, in issues, in policy. Instead, voters increasingly vote on the basis of "what's in it for me."

Joseph Schumpeter warned in 1918 that the fiscal state would in the end undermine government's ability to govern. Fifteen years later, Keynes hailed the fiscal state as the great liberator; no longer limited by restraints on spending, government in the fiscal state could govern effectively, Keynes maintained. We now know that Schumpeter was right.

The Megastate has been somewhat more successful in the social sphere than in the economic one. Still, it has not even earned a passing grade. Or rather, the social actions and policies that have worked well are those that by and large do not fit the doctrine of the Megastate. They are the social policies that follow earlier rules and earlier concepts. They are the social policies that *regulate* or the social policies that *provide*. They are not the social policies in which government becomes the doer. Those, with few exceptions, have not been successful.

In the British National Health Service, the part that pays physicians for patients on their lists works extremely well. But in the other part—where government manages hospitals and dispenses health care—there has been problem after problem. Costs are high and are going up as fast as health-care costs go up in any other country. Patients have to wait months and sometimes years for elective surgery to correct conditions that are serious but not life-threatening, whether a hip replacement, a prolapsed uterus, or a cataract in the eye. That during these months or years the patient is in pain and often disabled is irrelevant. As a doer, government has become so incompetent that the National Health Service is now encouraging hospitals to "contract out." Government will pay hospitals as it does physicians, but it will no longer manage them.

Equally instructive are the American policies of the War on Poverty which President Lyndon B. Johnson started with such good intentions in the 1960s. One of these programs has worked. It is Headstart, which pays independent and locally managed organizations to teach disadvantaged preschool children. None of the programs government itself runs has had results.

The most successful social policies of the last ten or fifteen years have been those in which governments—local governments primarily—"contract out," either to a business or to a non-profit agency. The number of such programs successfully contracted out is growing, and growing fast. Originally, services such as cleaning the streets were handled this way. Now the U.S. government is contracting out social programs like Headstart or the rehabilitation of youthful offenders. And, in the United States at least, we will increasingly contract out schooling, opting for "vouchers" under which the parents of a schoolchild can decide which school, public or even private, they want to send their children to, with the state paying the school of the parents' choice. In other words, we are beginning to apply to elementary education what we learned forty years ago from the G.I. Bill of Rights with respect to higher education. Government sets the rules, government sets the standards, government provides. But government does not *do*.

THE COLD WAR STATE—THE FAILURE OF SUCCESS

The Cold War State did not guarantee "peace": during the post–World War II years, there were as many "minor" conflicts as in any period of history, all over the world. But the Cold War State made possible the avoidance of major global war, not despite the tremendous military arsenal, but because of it.

The arms race made possible arms control. This resulted in the longest period without great power war in modern history. Fifty years have now gone by without military conflict between great powers. The peace settlement of the Congress of Vienna after the Napoleonic Wars—so celebrated by present-day "*real-politicians*" like Henry Kissinger—maintained great power peace for thirty-eight years, from 1815 until the outbreak of the Crimean War in 1853. Then, after almost twenty years of major conflicts—the American Civil War, the war between Prussia and Austria, the war between France and Germany—there were forty-three years, from 1871 to 1914, in which no great power fought another (except for the war between Japan and Russia in

1905; but Japan was not considered a great power until after that war). Only twenty-one years elapsed between World War I and World War II. The near-fifty years following 1945 in which no great power fought another great power is thus a record. Precisely because they had become Cold War states, the major powers could control armaments and thereby make sure that there was no such preponderance of military might as would tempt one of them to risk major conflict.

The best example is the Cuban missile crisis. It was largely caused by President John F. Kennedy's blunder in not standing up to Russia over the Berlin Wall and by his misjudgment and vacillation during the Bay of Pigs invasion of Cuba. This convinced Khrushchev that the United States would buckle down and accept the establishment of a Russian nuclear base in the western hemisphere. As soon as it became clear that the United States would not tolerate such provocation, however, the Russians retracted—and because Khrushchev had misjudged and thereby risked a major conflict with another great power, he was overthrown by his own military shortly thereafter.

The fifty years since the end of World War II have fully proven the basic assumptions on which the Cold War State was based. The weapons of modern warfare can no longer be produced in facilities that also produce the goods needed for peacetime. They cannot be produced by converting civilian facilities to wartime production as was still largely done in World War II. In turn, the facilities that produce the weapons of modern warfare—whether an aircraft carrier, a "smart bomb," or a guided missile—have to be built long before there is a war or even the threat of one.

If any proof of these assumptions had been needed, the 1991 war against Iraq provided it. None of the weapons which paralyzed what was one of the world's largest military forces, and which decided a war in the shortest time in which any war had ever been decided before (breaking the record established in 1866 when the Prussians knocked out the Austrians in four weeks), could have been produced in any peacetime facility. Each weapons system had required at least ten and in most cases fifteen years of work before it could become effective on the battlefield.

There is no going back, in other words, to the assumption on which the traditional nation-state was founded: that a small military force, augmented by reservists, is all that is needed to hold the field while civilian economic facilities are being converted to wartime production.

But the fifty years during which the Cold War State worked are also over. We need arms control now more than ever. There can be no return to "peace" if it is defined as the absence of military might. Innocence, once lost, can never be recovered. But the so-called Cold War State is no longer tenable. It no longer works.

The Cold War State has become economically self-destructive. The Soviet Union, as we have seen, succeeded in building an exceedingly powerful military force. But the burden this military force imposed became so intolerably heavy that it played a major part in the collapse of Soviet economy and Soviet society.

Now, that burden is becoming equally heavy for the United States. It is generally accepted that one of the main reasons why Japan and Germany have been doing so well economically while the United States has been falling behind is the cost of U.S. defense. The economic burden—5 or 6 percent of GNP—is the lesser problem. A far more severe problem is the diversion of the scarcest resources—trained engineers and scientists—to economically unproductive defense work. In the United States, 70 percent of all money spent on research and development is spent on defense work; in Japan, it is less than 5 percent. This conceals an even more important qualitative difference. Defense research in the United States has attracted the best and brightest of young engineers and scientists, thus starving the American economy of its most needed nourishment, knowledge. Where the ablest American engineers these last forty years have worked on "smart bombs," their Japanese counterparts have worked on perfecting the fax machine or taking the rattle out of an automobile door. Peacetime goods and wartime goods are no longer being produced by the same technologies, by the same processes, and in the same facilities. There is therefore no longer much, if any, "fall-out." The United States has spent enormous sums of money on the "technology transfer" from defense research to civilian products. The results have been close to zero.

Even worse were the effects of the Cold War State on economic development. There is very little doubt that Latin America rather than East Asia would have been the "economic miracle" of the 1960s and 1970s but for the fact that money and trained people in those countries were wasted on building up huge armed forces that had no military value.

A nation—even the richest—that spends in peacetime more than 2 or 2.5 percent of its GNP on armaments (still twice as much as Japan spends) cannot expect for very long to remain competitive in the world economy. It will be under increasing inflationary pressure. In fact, it should not even be considered *creditworthy*.

But even militarily, the Cold War State no longer works. In fact, the Cold War State can no longer guarantee arms control. Even small nations can no longer be prevented from building total-war capacity—whether nuclear, chemical, or biological. The worry over how to control the Soviet Union's nuclear arsenal as the empire disintegrates into individual nation-states is just one indication of this. So is the fact that any number of countries that are otherwise quite insignificant in terms of population or economic strength are rapidly acquiring nuclear, chemical, and biological warfare capacities; Iraq was one example, Libya is another, and so are Iran, North Korea, and Pakistan. These small countries could not, of course, win a war against a great power— as Iraq's Saddam Hussein still believed. But they can become international blackmailers and terrorists. With such countries as their base, small bands of adventurers (land-based pirates, in effect) could hold the world to ransom.

Arms control can thus no longer be exercised through the Cold War State as it was exercised for the half century after World War II. Unless arms control becomes transnational, it cannot be exercised at all—which would make global conflict practically inevitable, even if the major powers still manage to avoid a Hot War between themselves.

Unlike the fiscal state and the Nanny State, the Cold War State has not been a total failure. In fact, if the aim of national policy in the age of the absolute weapons can be said to be the avoidance of World War III, then it must be considered a success—the only success of the Megastate. But in the end this success has turned to failure, both economically and militarily.

The Megastate has reached a dead end. But, alas, there is no going back to yesterday's nation-state, as neo-Conservatives or economists of the Austrian School (such as Ludwig von Mises or Frederick Hayek) would have us believe. For new forces are rising that will both outflank and undermine the nation-state.

7

Transnationalism, Regionalism, and Tribalism

EVEN BEFORE WORLD WAR I, politicians and political scientists warned that the nation-state was becoming outmoded, and called instead for supranational institutions. In fact, the nineteenth century had already created quite a few. In earlier centuries, treaties were between one state and another; the nineteenth century wrote multinational treaties—one after the other. The first half of the century produced multinational conventions to stamp out piracy and the slave trade and to guarantee the Freedom of the Seas. The multinational treaties of the nineteenth century's second half—those setting up, for example, the International Postal Union and the International Red Cross—for the first time put in place non-national and, indeed, supranational agencies. Then, in the early years of the twentieth century, the International Court of Justice in The Hague was established and given jurisdiction over disputes between national states. These non-national or transnational treaties and agencies were, however, seen as dealing with "technical" matters, and thus not infringing on national sovereignty. (That was surely fiction. The International Red Cross was given the right to inspect prisonerof-war camps in wartime; and The Hague court held jurisdiction over boundary disputes between national states.)

After World War I, it became conventional wisdom that the nation-state was obsolete. This belief underlay the attempt to create the first avowedly supranational agency, the League of Nations. But it proved impotent right away. And the United Nations, set up after World War II, for its first forty years served primarily as an arena in which the superpowers fought each other. A post–World War II attempt to create a transnational currency was sponsored by John Maynard Keynes in the last months of his life. It was defeated by the Americans. In turn, the American proposal to transnationalize the atom—the Baruch Plan for transnational control of nuclear energy and nuclear arms—was rejected by the Russians. And the most successful of these post–World War II inventions, GATT (the General Agreement on Trade and Tariffs), while clearly meant to impose transnationalism in an area central to sovereignty, foreign trade, has rarely prevailed against national interests.

Instead, the period after World War II saw, first, an explosive growth in the number of nation-states as the successors to the prewar empires all organized themselves as such, and second, the mutation of the nation-state into the Megastate.

But in the last decades—beginning perhaps in the 1970s—the nation-state has begun to come apart. It has already been outflanked in crucial areas where "sovereignty" has lost all meaning. Increasingly, the new challenges facing every government are challenges that simply cannot be dealt with by national or even international action. They require *transnational* agencies, which have a "sovereignty" of their own. Increasingly, *regionalism* is also sidelining the nation-state. And internally, the nation-state is being undermined by *tribalism*.

MONEY KNOWS NO FATHERLAND . . .

"Money knows no fatherland" is a very old saying. But the nation-state was invented in large part to disprove it. Control over money was at the very center of what came to be called "sovereignty." But money has slipped the leash; it has gone transnational. It cannot be controlled any longer by national states, not even by their acting together.

No central bank any longer controls money flows. It can try to influence them by raising or lowering interest rates. But in the flow of money, political factors are increasingly as important as interest rates. The amount of money beyond the control of any one central bank, that is, the amount of money traded every day on the transnational markets (the New York foreign exchange market or the London interbank market), so greatly exceeds anything needed to finance national and international transactions that the flows escape any attempt to control or limit them, let alone manage them.

. . . NOR DOES INFORMATION

Information was not included among Bodin's attributes of sovereignty—there was not much of it in the late sixteenth century. But when the mass media emerged in this century, control of information was at once seen as essential by the new practitioners of national sovereignty, the totalitarians. Beginning with Lenin, every one of them—Mussolini, Stalin, Hitler—tried to exercise total control over information. And in the democratic countries, mastery of information (particularly in television) increasingly became the central art of politician and politics.

Today, information is fully as transnational as money. Governments can still control the news programs; but even in Germany during World War II, as many people may have listened clandestinely to the BBC as listened to Nazi propaganda chief Joseph Goebbels on the evening news. Yet news programs are an increasingly small part of "information." Any thirty-second advertisement, any eighteen-minute soap opera episode, contains as much information as the most carefully controlled news program—maybe more. There are no national boundaries any more for information. Surely the increasing inability of the most absolute regime in history to control access to information was a major factor in the collapse of Communism and the Soviet Empire.

Information may be distorted. The picture of American life conveyed by one of the world's most popular television programs, "Dallas," is not even a caricature. But that does not alter the fact that "Dallas" has been seen by more people in more countries than any other kind of "message." Even in Communist China, it could not be kept off the air. In a few years, with receiving dishes so small that no secret police could prevent their use inside the home, and with satellites overhead beaming programs to any point of the globe, information, for better or worse, will have become truly transnational and truly beyond the control of any one country. Countries concerned about the integrity of their own national culture (Japan, say, or France) will attempt to protect sovereign control of popular information. But such attempts are futile, it is abundantly clear.

It *may* be possible to restore control over money through a transnational institution. The European Community is proposing the establishment of a European Central Bank and a common currency. This would be tantamount to transnational control of economic and tax policy, which would reduce the national state in the economic sphere to the position of a local administrator. In respect to information, no such transnational institution is even possible—not even under a world dictatorship. Modern technology endows the individual with the means to circumvent totalitarian controls on information. Banning fax machines and copying machines was still attempted by the Communists in their last desperate attempt to maintain control of information. It led only to underground publication of the *samizdat*, manuscripts copied by hand by hundreds or thousands of students and circulated freely throughout the Soviet Union. Once people have personal computers, fax machines, telephones, copiers, and videocassette recorders in their possession and in their homes (let alone television receivers, which can pluck messages from any satellite overhead), there is no way to reestablish control over information.

Money going transnational outflanks the nation-state by nullifying national economic policy. Information going transnational outflanks the nation-state by undermining (in fact, destroying) the identification of "national" with "cultural" identity. What does it mean to be a Frenchman if most of them prefer Charlie Chaplin to any play written by a French writer and produced in France?, a critic asked when movies first made their appearance in the 1920s. But now French people—and English, German, Russian, Japanese, and Chinese—prefer Charlie Chaplin's successors, the situation comedies or the "docudramas," to anything produced in their own countries. "High culture" has gone supranational fully as much as "popular culture." Architecture surely conveys as much of a message as does a TV show or a news bulletin; and today there is very little difference between the office buildings that go up in Tokyo and those that go up in Dallas or Düsseldorf.

TRANSNATIONAL NEEDS: THE ENVIRONMENT

There is a growing need for truly transnational institutions, that is, for institutions that in their own sphere transcend the nation-state. These institutions can—indeed, they must—make decisions and take action in a wide range of areas, cutting through the barrier of sovereignty and directly controlling citizens and organizations within a nation-state. These decisions push aside the nation-state or turn it into an agent of the transnational institution.

The first is the environment. Local action is necessary to prevent destructive pollution. But the biggest threat to the environment is not local pollution—whether the effluents of a nearby paper mill, the wastes spewed into the ocean by municipal sewage, or the runoff of pesticides and fertilizers from local farms. The greatest threat is damage to the human habitat, to the atmosphere, to the tropical forests which are the earth's lungs, to the earth's oceans, to its water supply, and to the air—the very environment on which all of humanity depends. And there is the pressing need to balance protection of the environment against the demands of the developing world, with its rapidly growing population.

These are not challenges which can be tackled within the borders of a national state. Pollution knows no boundaries, any more than money and information do.

The forests of Scandinavia, which may be Europe's greatest natural resource, are being destroyed by pollution generated in the English Midlands and Scotland, in Belgium and eastern Germany. Acid rain, which similarly threatens the forests of Canada—maybe the greatest natural resource of North America—is generated in the American Midwest. But maintaining the Amazon rain forest in effect means putting severe short-term limitations on the ability of a growing Brazilian population to feed itself. Who will pay for this, and how?

STAMPING OUT TERRORISM

Second only to the environment is the growing need for transnational action and institutions to abort the return of private armies and stamp out terrorism. The military action against Iraq in the winter and spring of 1991 may have been a starting point. The Iraqi invasion itself was a threat only to a very small number of countries; it was *not* a threat to the United States, by the way, nor to any other of the developed countries. Yet for the first time in recorded history, practically all the nation-states acted together to put down an act of terrorism—for this is what the Iraqi invasion of Kuwait represented.

Today, private armies have returned, after a gap of nearly four hundred years. During the seventeenth century, Japan (around 1600), and Europe fifty years later, decided that the nation-state alone could be allowed to maintain a military force. But with nuclear explosives, chemical weapons, and biological weapons, private armies have once again become possible. Terrorism is all the more threatening as very small groups can effectively hold even large countries to ransom. A nuclear bomb can easily be put into a locker or a postal box in any major city and exploded by remote control; so could a bacterial bomb, containing enough anthrax spores to kill thousands of people and to contaminate a big city's water supply, making it uninhabitable.

Twenty years ago, many countries, especially the Communist countries, thought that terrorism could be used as a tool of national policy. There is little doubt, for instance, that the terrorist groups in West Germany were recruited, financed, and trained in East Germany. Or that Iraq, Iran, Syria, and Libya all recruited, financed, and trained groups to terrorize the Western world, and particularly the United States.

By now most countries—though by no means all—have realized that this is counterproductive. But lack of support for terrorism is not enough. What is needed to control the threat of terrorism is action that goes beyond any one sovereign state. There is a precedent: the nineteenth-century treaties which stamped out the slave trade and made piracy on the high seas a transnational offense.

ARMS CONTROL

Third—and closely connected with the stamping out of terrorism—is the need for transnational arms control, which was discussed in the preceding chapter.

Finally, will there be a transnational agency to monitor and to enforce human rights? Should there be such an agency? Would a transnational agency, for instance, have been able to prevent Hitler's Holocaust? Or the "ethnic cleansing" of Moslems and Croats carried out by the Serbs in the former Yugoslavia? Or the horror of Somalia? Jimmy Carter as U.S. president in the 1970s clearly favored such an agency. What might actually bring it about is the threat to prosperous countries of being inundated by millions of refugees unless transnational action can put an end to racial, religious, political, and ethnic persecution.

We may already have moved further toward transnationalism than most of us—and especially most politicians—realize. In respect to the environment, we are close to transnational action to prevent, or at least to slow down, ozone depletion and the "green-house effect" of worldwide warming. We are close to transnational action to protect the world's great oceans and their resources. Already there is a multilateral treaty to protect Antarctica.

With respect to terrorism and arms control, the turning point may indeed have been the Gulf war, and especially the decision to entrust the destruction of Iraq's terror weapons (nuclear, chemical, and biological) to agencies of the United Nations rather than to have this task carried out by the victorious U.S. Army. Even earlier, in a step that was totally unprecedented—and indeed ran counter to all earlier American legal principles—the U.S. government proposed an International Criminal Court, with direct jurisdiction over acts of terrorism committed anywhere. And the new government of the Russian Republic has revived the original Baruch Plan of 1947, proposing to hand over control of all nuclear weapons worldwide to a transnational agency—which, in effect, would then result in the elimination of all nuclear weapons and in action to stop any attempt by any country to build nuclear arms facilities.

The design of the necessary agencies is still ahead of us; so is the speed with which any of them will develop. It may well take major catastrophes to make national governments willing to accept subordination to such institutions and their decisions. The development of transnational institutions, the decision as to spheres in which they can act, their constitution, their powers, their relationship to national governments, and their financing (should they, for instance, have taxing power of their own?) are still far off. We are indeed completely unprepared—as witness the ludicrous wrangling over who should pay what share of the costs of the military action in Iraq in 1991. But it is predictable that the design and construction of transnational institutions will be a central political issue for many decades to come. This means that the *limitation of sovereignty* will become a central issue in international relations, and in foreign as well as domestic politics.

REGIONALISM: THE NEW REALITY

Internationalism is no longer Utopia; it is already on the horizon—if barely so. Regionalism is already a reality. Regionalism does not create a superstate whose government *replaces* national government. Rather, it creates regional governing agencies that sideline national government in important areas and make it increasingly irrelevant.

The trend toward regionalism was triggered by the European Community (EC). But it will not be confined to it. The European Community started out as the European *Economic* Community, that is, as a purely economic organization. It has assumed more and more political functions, and is now proposing the creation of a central bank and a European currency. But it also has taken jurisdiction over access to trades and professions: over mergers, acquisitions, and cartels; over social legislation; over everything that can possibly be construed as "non-tariff barriers" to the free movement of goods, services, and people. It is moving toward a European army.

The European Community then triggered the attempt to create a North American economic community, built around the United States but integrating both Canada and Mexico into a common market. So far this attempt is purely economic in its goal. But it can hardly remain so in the long run.

What makes this so important is that the impetus for the North American economic community did not come from the United States; it came from Mexico. Yet for over one hundred fifty years, ever since Mexico was unified under the presidency of Benito Juárez, the goal of Mexican policy has been to put as much distance as possible between its country and its pushy and totally alien neighbor to the north. No two contiguous countries in the world are as different as Mexico and the United States—in language, in religion, but above all in culture, values, and tradition. Yet Mexico had to accept in the end that the one hundred fifty years of isolationist policy had ended in failure; in order to survive as a country and civilization, it has to integrate itself, at least economically, with the huge, dangerous, and alien neighbor to the north.

The treaty which the Mexican government has proposed to establish a customs union between Mexico and the other two North American countries, the United States and Canada, may fail to go through. But the economic integration of the three countries into one region is proceeding so fast that it will make little difference whether the marriage is sanctified legally or not.

The same will increasingly be true in East Asia; the only question is whether there will be one or several such economic regions. There might be a region in which Coastal China and the countries of Southeast Asia coalesce around Japan. It is possible also that rapidly growing Coastal China, which embraces about two fifths of China's population and produces about two thirds of China's GNP—from Tientsin in the north to Canton in the south—will establish itself as one region, with a Japan-oriented Southeast Asia as a second region.

Which route Asia chooses will be among the key questions of the 1990s and into the early years of the twenty-first century.

There is also a growing movement toward "mini-regions." No sooner did the Soviet Empire disintegrate than "Turkic" successor states in Central Asia proposed a "Turkic Region," centered in the most Westernized and most highly developed Turkic country—Turkey. No sooner did the three Baltic countries—Lithuania, Latvia, and Estonia—secede from the Soviet Empire than they began to talk of a "Baltic Region," in which they would join with their Scandinavian neighbors—and above all Finland and Sweden. A similar mini-region embracing the peoples and nations of Southeast Asia (Malaysia, Singapore, Indonesia, the Philippines, and Thailand) has been proposed by the prime minister of Malaysia. And an economic region replacing the old Soviet Union is what Russia's prime minister is pushing and hoping for.

But whether there are three or four or more such regions is less important than that the thrust toward regionalism is irreversible. It is also inevitable as a response to the new economic reality.

In the knowledge economy, neither traditional protectionism nor traditional free trade can work by themselves. What is needed is an economic unit that is big enough to establish meaningful free trade and strong competition within the unit. This unit has to be large enough to allow new "high-tech" industries to develop with a high degree of protection. And the reason for this lies in the nature of high tech, that is, of knowledge industry.

High-tech industry does not follow the supply–demand equations of classical, neo-classical, and Keynesian economics. There, the costs of production go up in proportion to the volume of production. In high-tech industries, by contrast, the costs of production go *down* very fast as the volume of production goes up—what is now called the "learning curve" (see Chapter 10 below).

The significance of this is that a high-tech industry can establish itself in such a way that it will destroy any competition—what I once called "adversarial trade." Once this has happened, there is almost no chance for the defeated industry to come back; it has ceased to exist. At the same time, however, the new high-tech industry has to have sufficient competition and challenge, or else it will simply not grow and develop. It will become monopolistic and lazy, and will soon be obsolete. The knowledge economy requires, therefore, economic units that are substantially larger than even a fair-sized national state; otherwise there will be no competition. But it also requires the ability to protect industry and to conduct trade with other trading blocs on the basis of reciprocity rather than either protection or free trade. This is an unprecedented situation. It makes regionalism both inevitable and irreversible.

But regionalism, as the example of the European Community shows, is not simply "international." It has to establish transnational, indeed supranational institutions.

The various regions as they are emerging are quite dissimilar. The European Community is built around a small nucleus of countries—the United Kingdom, Germany, France, Italy, and Spain—which are roughly comparable in size and population, and which, despite great differences in wealth, are still ranged along a continuum of economic development. The most advanced Spanish company, for instance, is actually more advanced than the average German company.

The North American economic community would be very different. In population, its three partners range from 250 million people in the United States to one tenth that number in Canada. The three differ widely in economic development. Parts of the United States are the world's wealthiest areas, whereas parts of Mexico (especially the south) are among the world's poorest and least developed.

The economic regions in Asia will be even more different. They will not even all share a common cultural heritage— Indonesia or Malaysia never were part of Confucian culture.

But they will all create large free trade areas, larger than free trade areas have ever been before. At the same time, they will create large areas that are unified in their response to the outside world and capable of being "reciprocal," that is, of being at the same time both wide open and protectionist.

These regions will not *replace* the nation-state. But they will sideline it.

THE RETURN OF TRIBALISM

Internationalism and regionalism challenge the sovereign nation-state from the outside. Tribalism undermines it from within. It saps the nation-state's integrating power. In fact, it threatens to replace nation with tribe.

In the United States, tribalism manifests itself in the growing emphasis on diversity rather than on unity. America has always been a country of immigrants. Every immigrant group was at first considered "foreign" and was discriminated against until two generations later when it had become "mainstream," beginning with the Irish in the 1830s and 1840s. America was a "melting pot." In the last thirty years, this has become highly unfashionable. Now "diversity" is the message preached and practiced. Any attempt to make new groups into "Americans" is considered discrimination; yet only sixty years ago the attempt to prevent such groups from becoming "Americans" would have been discrimination. Whether the new groups are Europeans or Asians, whether they are black, brown, or white, whether they are Catholics or Buddhists, the emphasis now is on maintaining their identities and preventing their being encouraged, let alone forced, to become "Americans."

This is by no means an American phenomenon and cannot even be explained in purely American terms (though clearly, as with everything in American society, the basic American problem, race relations between white and black, is central to the phenomenon). Tribalism is even more rampant in Europe. It has torn asunder Yugoslavia in bloody civil war. It threatens civil war all over the former Soviet Empire. Scots want to secede from the United Kingdom; Slovaks demand autonomy and separation from the Czechs; Belgium is torn by strife between the Flemish and the French-speaking Walloons. Tiny local groups, though never discriminated against, demand "cultural autonomy"—for example, the 150,000 Sorbs living in the woods south of Berlin who are the last survivors of the Slavic tribes that inhabited Northern Germany more than a thousand years ago.

Tribalism as a phenomenon has become worldwide. Will Canada survive this century, or will it split into two parts, an English-speaking and a French-speaking one? Or even into four parts: a French-speaking Quebec; an English-speaking Ontario and Manitoba; the Prairie Provinces; and British Columbia? (Where then would the Maritimes go? And Newfoundland?) Will India remain united politically? Will Corsica and Brittany stay within France? Will the Lapps in Northern Finland and Northern Sweden gain autonomy? Will Mexico stay united—or will the Indian south break away from the Hispanic north? The list is endless.

One reason for the trend toward tribalism is that bigness no longer confers much advantage. In the age of nuclear war, not even the biggest country can defend its citizens. And the smallest one—Israel is a case in point—can build terror weapons.

Now that money and information have become transnational, even very small units are economically viable. Big or small, everyone has equal access to money and information, on the same terms. Indeed, the true "success stories" of the last thirty years have been very small countries.

In the 1920s, the Austrian republic, remnant of the old Austro-Hungarian Empire, was universally considered much too small to be economically viable, with fewer than 6 million inhabitants. In fact, this was the main argument in favor of Hitler's annexation of the country in Austria itself. The Austria of the 1920s and 1930s was indeed in pitiful economic shape, with chronic unemployment of up to 20 percent. Post–World War II Austria is hardly larger. In addition, it had lost the trading area it still possessed in the twenties, the successor states to the former Austria-Hungary, which had become Communist. Yet post–World War II Austria has developed into one of Europe's most prosperous countries.

So have Finland—equally small—and Sweden, and Switzerland. Hong Kong and Singapore have done even better. Twenty years ago, the most fervent nationalist in any of the three Baltic countries which Stalin had annexed in 1940 would not have believed that his country could survive economically on its own; now few doubt it. And the same is true of Canadian Quebec.

After all, a small country can now join an economic region and thus get the best of two worlds: cultural and political independence, and economic integration. It is surely no coincidence that tiny Luxembourg has proved the most fervent "European" of them all.

THE NEED FOR ROOTS

The main reason for tribalism is neither politics nor economics. It is existential. People need roots in a transnational world; they need community.

All educated people in Spain know Castilian (which the outside world calls Spanish). But the language many Spaniards speak in school and at home and, increasingly, even in the office is Catalan or Basque or Galician or Andalusian. The change may be a change in emphasis, but it does represent a fundamental change in identity. Catalans, Basques, Galicians, Andalusians see the same soap operas on their TV sets. The products they buy are as likely to have been made in Japan or in the United States as in Spain. Increasingly, they work for an employer whose headquarters are in Tokyo, in South Korea, in New York, or in Düsseldorf. They live increasingly in a transnational world. But they feel the need for local roots; the need to belong to a local community.

Tribalism is not the opposite of transnationalism; it is its *pole*. More and more American Jews marry outside their faith; but this is then the reason why they come to emphasize their Jewish roots and the culture of Judaism. In the forty years since World War II, there have been more and more Serb boys who married Croatian girls—and conversely more and more Serb girls who married Bosnian Muslims or Croatians. But this only made the rest of the Serbs, Croats, and Bosnians more conscious of their tribal identities. Welsh and Irish marry more and more English people, only to become more conscious of being Welsh and Irish. Tribalism thrives precisely because people increasingly realize that what happens in Osaka affects people in Slovenia who have no idea where Osaka is and can hardly find it on the map. Precisely because the world has become transnational in so many ways—and must become ever more so—people need to define themselves in terms they can understand. They need a geographic, a linguistic, a religious, and a cultural community which is visible to them and which, to use an old cliché, they can "get their arms around."

The Sorbs in the woods outside of Berlin do not cease to be part of Germany and German culture. But they also see themselves—and demand to be seen—as something distinct. The Latin American immigrants into Los Angeles—whether from Mexico or Central America—become American citizens as soon as they possibly can. They expect to have the same opportunities as native-born Americans have. They expect their children to receive the same access to education, to careers, to jobs. But they also expect to be able to maintain their Hispanic identity, Hispanic culture, and a Hispanic community. The more transnational the world becomes, the more tribal it will also be.

This undermines the very foundations of the nation-state. In fact, it ceases to be a "nation-state," and becomes a "state" plain and simple, an administrative rather than a political unit.

Internationalism, regionalism, and tribalism between them are rapidly creating a new polity, a new and complex political structure, without precedent. To use a mathematical metaphor, the post-capitalist polity has three vectors, each pulling in a different direction. But an equation with three vectors has no one solution.

In the meantime, as the old English saying has it, "the work of government must go on." The only institutions we have so far for this work are those of the nation-state and its government. The first political task of the post-capitalist polity must be to restore the performance capacity of government, which the Megastate has so seriously diminished.

8

The Needed Government
Turnaround

T HE NEXT DECADES will make unprecedented demands on
political courage, political imagination, political innovation,
political leadership. They will demand high government competence. The demands will be *external* ones as well as *internal*
ones.

Externally, there is a need for new thinking and radical
innovations in several areas: the relationship between national
governments and transnational tasks; between national governments and regional organizations; and between new but also very
different regions. The next decades should—for the first time—
see the emergence of political institutions transcending the
nation-state, and of transnational law. The designers and
builders of these new institutions, and the drafters of this transnational law, will have to be national governments and national
politicians.

Internally, there is an equally demanding and equally urgent
need to make government effective again—despite the transformation of society into a pluralism of organizations, and despite
the near collapse of government's capacity to make decisions

under the pressure of special-interest groups and the "tyranny of the small minority."

The great fear of the eighteenth-century political thinkers— for example, the framers of the American Constitution—was the fear of "factions," special-interest groups with a tendency to make their own interest or issue a "moral imperative" to which everything else is subordinated. The brilliant answer to this fear was the party. It was invented simultaneously, though independently, in Britain, the United States, and France in the two decades between 1815 and 1835 in which so much of the modern world came into being.

The party transcended faction. In Europe, it was organized around a vague ideology, a "program." In the United States, it was organized around equally broad and vague "interests." But whatever its professed rationale, the party was organized for a common purpose: to gain and to hold political power. It was organized to *govern*.

It therefore had to attract the voters in the middle, had to eschew extremes and be willing to compromise. It had to confine its actions, when in power, to measures that would command support way beyond its own adherents, that is, actions that would be acceptable to that part of the "middle" that had not voted for it. The clearest expression of this principle is the provision in the American Constitution regarding the presidential veto, which can be overridden only by two thirds of both houses of the Congress. This means that it can be overridden only if substantial members of both parties agree on a measure, which forces both Congress and president to stay in the middle.

Today, parties are in tatters everyplace. The ideologies that enabled European parties to bring together disparate factions into one organization to gain and control power have lost most of their integrating power. The parties and their slogans make no sense to voters, especially younger ones. The traditional interest groups of the United States are largely gone; where are the farmers, the workers, the small businessmen, on whom Mark Hanna based the Republican Party in 1896, and who were then taken over in 1932 by Franklin D. Roosevelt to forge the new Democratic Party?

Governments have thus become powerless against the onslaught of special-interest groups, have indeed become powerless to govern—to make decisions and to enforce them.

It has become fashionable these last years to be "antigovernment." But this won't work. We need strong, effective government. In fact, we can expect more rather than less government in the next decades. The new tasks—protection of the environment; stamping out private armies and international terrorism; making arms control effective—all will require more rather than less government. But they will require *a different form of government.*

In the last fifteen to twenty years, one political leader after the other has come into power vowing to "cut back government" or to "fight the insiders." The first one to be elected on such a platform was Jimmy Carter in the United States, followed by Ronald Reagan, who in turn was followed by another "antigovernment" candidate, George Bush. In the United Kingdom, Margaret Thatcher was elected on an "anti-government" platform and governed on it for ten years.

In every case, the results have been pitiful. Government expenditures and government regulations have increased faster than ever before under these so-called anti-government leaders. Spending under them has gotten totally out of control. And the more these governments spent, the less competent and less potent they became. Government did not "grow"; it became obese and paralyzed by its own overweight.

No administration in American history has run a larger deficit than that of President Bush. According to accepted wisdom, that should have made impossible any kind of recession. In fact, the enormous jumps in government spending and government deficits during the first three years of the Bush administration brought about the deepest and longest recession the United States has suffered since World War II. Prime Minister Thatcher—arguably the ablest and surely the most determined political leader of the so-called Free World since General de Gaulle—similarly had little to show but growing deficits for her attempts to cut government back, to make it more effective and competent, and to turn around the British economy.

This is just as true for France. President François Mitterand dramatically increased French government expenditures—without achieving any results. Under his presidency, France has steadily lost ground as an economic and industrial power. And in Japan, the very ability to govern is being undermined by perpetual scandals which are the direct result of the "pork-barrel state."

Yet only national governments and their political leaders can do the jobs that have to be done. They alone have *legitimacy*.

Government therefore has to regain a modicum of performance capacity. It has to be *turned around*. The term itself is a business one. But to turn around any institution—whether a business, a labor union, a university, a hospital, or a government—requires always the same three steps:

(1) Abandonment of the things that do not work, the things that have never worked; the things that have outlived their usefulness and their capacity to contribute;

(2) Concentration on the things that do work, the things that produce results, the things that improve the organization's ability to perform; and

(3) Analysis of the half-successes, the half-failures. A turn-around requires abandoning whatever does not perform and doing more of whatever does perform.

THE FUTILITY OF MILITARY AID

If one were to rank the policies of the Megastate in order of their futility, military aid would surely be at the top of the things that have never worked, and therefore first on the list of things to abandon. Military aid goes back to hoary antiquity. The Roman historians already pointed out that the military aid the king of Persia gave to Sparta in its war against Athens only made it possible, a few decades later, for the Macedonians to gain domination over Greece and thus to give Alexander the Great the army and the arms to overthrow the Persian Empire.

But surely military aid has never been used more extensively—and more unsuccessfully—than in the years of the Megastate, the years since World War II. It has backfired practically without exception. Examples are the military aid the United States gave Iran under the Shah; the military aid the Soviet Union gave to Afghanistan; the military aid the United States gave to Iraq. Nor has the military aid given to any number of Latin American generals been any more productive; it succeeded only in making the generals rich and their countries poor.

To support a country that is under attack by a powerful enemy is one thing. To give military aid to "friendly" regimes is quite another. This is extortion money—and it only increases the extortionist's appetite. To the threat: "If you don't give us these planes, these tanks, these missiles, we'll get them elsewhere," the proper answer is: "Go right ahead." And the oft-invoked need to maintain a "military balance" in a region is pure sham. In no instance during the last forty years has military aid stabilized a region; it has only stepped up the arms race.

The idea of military aid is in itself a poor one. Military aid does not create reliable allies. In all probability the aid recipients will turn against the aid giver—as Iran and Iraq turned against the United States and as Afghanistan turned against the Soviet Union. One reason is that recipients increasingly resent being dependent the more aid they receive. Another, more important, reason is that the aid giver becomes identified with the government to which the aid is being given. Even if the aid is not being used to keep a government in power, the aid giver is increasingly seen as the supporter of the incumbents: of the Colonels in Greece, for instance, or of the Shah of Iran. When the incumbents are removed, even by peaceful means, the successor government is almost forced to turn against the foreign power that worked with its predecessors, that is, against the aid giver.

Military aid has done damage both to the countries that extended it and to the recipients. It forces the recipient to misdirect its vision, its resources, its energies toward military ends, and to neglect everything else. Again and again, it has created military dictators. And far too many of them then became international terrorists, who used the military aid they received to turn their country into a pirate base from which to terrorize the international community—as Saddam Hussein did in Iraq.

The only people likely to be hurt if military aid is abandoned are the defense contractors.

WHAT TO ABANDON IN ECONOMIC THEORY

Economic aid has been hotly debated these last years. Has it actually aided the recipients or has it weakened them? There is substance to the charge that food aid such as the United States has provided in huge quantities has allowed governments— especially in Africa—to neglect their own agriculture and to impoverish their own farmers. All told, government-to-government aid, that invention of the 1950s, has had at best marginal results. Not much more can be said for the grants or loans made by or through such quasi-governmental institutions as the World Bank; few of them have provided substantial development. Still, the idea of economic aid may be a good one, though we obviously do not yet know how to do it.

If we have learned one thing, it is that government cannot manage the economic "weather." Government cannot effectively prevent or overcome short-term economic fluctuations such as a recession. No one before 1929 expected government to be able to manage the economic weather. Since then, every government in every country has promised to be able to cure recessions. But this is pure quackery; no government has so far been able to deliver on such a promise. Political leaders will have to learn to tell their constituents: "No one knows how to manage the economy short term any more than the physician knows how to cure the common cold. We'd better keep our hands off it."

A corollary to this, however, is that government does need to regain the ability to avoid major depressions. Government spending to increase consumption has proven ineffectual here: wherever tried, the public hoards the added purchasing power rather than spending it. The last time this happened in the United States was during Jimmy Carter's presidency. But it has happened regularly in every earlier such attempt since the first one, Franklin D. Roosevelt's attempt to cure the Great Depression by government creation of purchasing power. The result was the severe economic collapse of 1936–37.

The one effective way to counteract a depression—that is, a prolonged period of structural change—is through investment in the infrastructure; and after prolonged boom periods, the infrastructure (roads, bridges, harbors, public buildings, public lands) is always in bad repair. For governments to be able to finance such investments requires that they operate with a balanced budget during good times—and during recessions as well. They will then have the ability to raise money, especially through borrowing, when there is need to do so. In other words, governments have to learn again to keep deficits as the weapon of last resort. In peacetime, deficits should be used—if at all—only to finance permanent improvements of the economy's wealth-generating capacity.

In the economic sphere, we need to abandon the theory of the fiscal state on which the Megastate has been operating, especially in the English-speaking world. We need to turn from a social policy of taxation back to an economic policy of taxation. To be sure, taxation has to be tempered by considerations of equity and justice. To be sure, there is room for taxation which penalizes, even harshly, socially undesirable activities, whether this be child labor or grossly excessive executive salaries such as have become the norm in American business in the last twenty or twenty-five years. But these are qualifiers. The center of tax policy has to be a *socially neutral* policy.

Is any of this politically feasible? The answer is yes; it is just not easy.

To abandon anything is always bitterly resisted. People in any organization, including bureaucrats and politicians, are always attached to the obsolete; the obsolescent; the things that should have worked but didn't; the things that once were productive and no longer are. They are most attached to what in an earlier book I called "investments in managerial ego."* But it is also always in such areas and in such ventures that the largest number of people—and usually the ablest ones—are employed. Every organization tends to deploy its ablest people to deal with "problems" rather than results—and especially an organization in trouble.

Abandoning anything is thus difficult—but only for a fairly short spell. Six months after such efforts have been abandoned, everybody wonders: "Why did it take us so long?"

The belief that the fiscal state can effectively redistribute income, and thereby reform society through taxation and subsidies, has been decisively disproven. The least egalitarian countries are those that have tried hardest to redistribute income: the Soviet Union; the United States; Great Britain. All they accomplished was to give us the "pork-barrel state"—the most dangerous degenerative disease that the body politic is suffering from. So far no one knows how we can get rid of this legalized looting of the commonwealth. It may require constitutional innovations—perhaps a new public agency independent of both legislature and executive, which audits spending proposals and determines whether this or that proposed outlay is actually in the public interest and compatible with public policy. (Such an audit would resemble in the public sphere the "business audit" proposed in Chapter 3 for the governance of corporations.) The idea will be called naive, not to say Utopian. Legislatures can be expected to resist any attempt to discipline themselves.

But in truth a good many legislators all over the world would welcome such an outside check on their undiscipline. They can-

* *Managing for Results* (1964).

not apply it themselves—or believe they cannot do so—without being punished by the special-interest groups. But they also know that the pork-barrel process is undermining their own positions and their standing with their constituents, quite apart from destroying their self-respect. In every country, money for government spending will become increasingly scarce in the years to come. This might make the control of pork-barrel spending increasingly attractive. That it is badly needed, no one doubts any more.

Abandonment comes first in the turnaround strategy. Until it has been accomplished, nothing else gets done. All resources are still being allocated to the "problems." The acrimonious and emotional debate over what to abandon holds everybody in its grip. There are those who argue that it is worth "just one more try." There are others who seek (fruitlessly) for a "compromise." There are the charlatans who promise to be able to amputate a gangrenous limb without inflicting pain; and so on. Until abandonment is out of the way, no work gets done.

CONCENTRATING ON WHAT DOES WORK

Rebirth can begin once the dead are buried. It starts by asking: What has been successful? Where have we had results? What should we concentrate on?

The economic performances of Japan and Germany during the past forty years both teach the same lesson. These countries focused on the economic "climate" instead of on the economic "weather." The aim of their economic policies—to turn to a different metaphor—has not been to make the patient *feel* good. It has been to make the patient healthy and to keep the patient healthy. It has been to create an economic environment in which the economy can grow; acquire resistance to infection, injury, and disease; acquire the ability to adapt and to change rapidly; and stay competitive.

Both countries almost immediately lost momentum, however, as soon as they attempted to "control the weather." The German economy began to drift in 1989 when the government—in order to buy the votes of the newly reunified East Germans—switched to massive deficit spending to jack up consumption. The attempt of the Japanese to offset short-term export contraction following the devaluation of the U.S. dollar in the mid-eighties by pushing up domestic consumer spending almost immediately triggered a runaway speculative boom in stock market and real estate prices. All it did was to create the "bubble economy," which then finally burst in 1991 and 1992.

Creating the right climate is not the same thing as keeping taxes low. The contention of the supply-side economists that low taxes by themselves guarantee economic health and growth has not been proven. Their contention that high taxes inevitably mean economic stagnation has been decisively disproven. Japan has had very high income tax rates all along. The incidence of taxation, as said earlier, is more important than the rate of taxation.

The proper aim of fiscal policy has to be the encouragement of investment in knowledge and in human resources, in productive facilities in business, and in infrastructure. This has been the secret of all the economic successes of the last half century, for Japan, for Germany, and for the "Four Asian Tigers": South Korea, Hong Kong, Singapore, and Taiwan. All were successful as long as they stuck to policies that focused on creating the economic climate and as long as they largely ignored the economic weather.

THE HALF-SUCCESSES: BEYOND THE NANNY STATE

The last step in a turnaround strategy is to look at the policies and activities that have been partially successful and partially unsuccessful. One tries to determine what precisely has been unsuccessful, so that one can stop doing it. Once again, the first question is: What should be abandoned? But then one has to ask: And what works? What should we be doing more of?

These questions have already been discussed in respect to one manifestation of the Megastate: the "Cold War State." Arms control has worked, in part; the Cold War State has not. What is needed now is transnational arms control. Arms control through "mutually assured destruction," that is, international arms control, has proven economically unbearable even for the richest nation, and militarily powerless to halt the spread of terror arms and their proliferation.

There is a second sphere in which the results have been mixed: the social sphere. The Nanny State itself has had few results. Very little has been achieved by government as the *doer* in the social sphere. But where we have had non-governmental action by autonomous community organizations, we have achieved a great deal. The post-capitalist society and the post-capitalist polity require a new *social sector*—both to satisfy social needs and to restore a meaningful sense of citizenship and community.

This, however, is such an important and novel subject that it deserves a chapter of its own.

9

Citizenship Through the Social Sector

SOCIAL NEEDS WILL GROW IN TWO AREAS. They will grow, first, in what has traditionally been considered *charity*: helping the peer, the disabled, the helpless, the victims. And they will grow, perhaps even faster, in respect to services that aim at *changing the community* and at *changing people*.

In a transition period, the number of people in need always grows. There are the huge masses of refugees all over the globe, victims of war and social upheaval, of racial, ethnic, political, and religious persecution, of government incompetence and of government cruelty. Even in the most settled and stable societies people will be left behind in the shift to knowledge work. It takes a generation or two before a society and its population catch up with radical changes in the composition of the work force and in the demands for skills and knowledge. It takes some time—the best part of a generation, judging by historical experience—before the productivity of service workers can be raised sufficiently to provide them with a "middle-class" standard of living.

The needs will grow equally—perhaps even faster—in the

second area of social services, services which do not dispense charity but attempt to make a difference in the community and to change people. Such services were practically unknown in earlier times, whereas charity has been with us for millennia. But they have mushroomed in the last hundred years, especially in the United States.

These services will be needed even more urgently in the next decades. One reason is the rapid increase in the number of elderly people in all developed countries, most of whom live alone and want to live alone. A second reason is the growing sophistication of health care and medical care, calling for health care research, health care education, and for more and more medical and hospital facilities. Then there is the growing need for continuing education of adults, and the need created by the growing number of one-parent families. The community service sector is likely to be one of the true "growth sectors" of developed economies, whereas we can hope that the need for charity will eventually subside again.

THE NEED TO "OUTSOURCE"

The attempt to satisfy all these needs through the Nanny State has largely failed—or at least as an attempt to have government run and manage these services. The first conclusion from the experience of the Nanny State is therefore for government to stop being a doer and manager in the social sphere and to confine itself to being the policy maker. This means that in the social sphere, as in the economic sphere, there is need to "contract out," to "outsource," to "unbundle." Just as we are restructuring the business enterprise by contracting out support work, clerical work, and maintenance work, so government needs to be restructured by contracting out work in the social sector.

There is an additional reason for contracting out social tasks: the need to raise the productivity of service work. Government is the largest employer of service workers; yet service workers in government have the lowest productivity. As long as they are government employees, their productivity cannot go up. A government agency must of necessity act like a bureaucracy. It must (indeed it should) subordinate productivity to rules and regulations. It must be wrapped in "red tape." It must focus on proper paperwork rather than on results. Otherwise it soon becomes a gang of thieves. And the largest single number of government employees in all developed countries are employed to deliver such services; to run such services; to doing in the social sector.

Contracting out is equally necessary to get the social tasks done. None of the U.S. programs of the last forty years in which we tried to tackle a social problem through government action has produced significant results. But independent non-profit agencies *have* had impressive results. Public schools in inner cities—for example, New York, Detroit, and Chicago—have been going downhill at an alarming rate. Church-run schools (especially schools of the Roman Catholic dioceses) have had startling successes—in the same communities, and with children from similarly broken families and of similar racial and ethnic groups. The only successes in fighting alcoholism and drug abuse (very substantial ones) have been achieved by such independent organizations as Alcoholics Anonymous, the Salvation Army, and the Samaritans. The only successes in getting "welfare mothers"— single mothers, often black or Hispanic—off welfare and back into paid work and a stable family life have been achieved by autonomous, non-profit organizations such as the Judson Center in Royal Oak, Michigan.* Improvements in major health care areas such as the prevention and treatment of cardiac disease and of mental illness have largely been the work of independent non-profit organizations. The American Heart Association and the American Mental Health Association, for instance, have sponsored the necessary research and taken the lead in educating both the medical community and the public in prevention and treatment.

* On this, see *Managing the Non-Profit Organization.*

To foster autonomous community organizations in the social sector is therefore an important step in turning government around and making it perform again.

But the greatest contribution that the autonomous community organization makes is as a new *center of meaningful citizenship.* The Megastate has all but destroyed citizenship. To restore it, the post-capitalist polity needs a "third sector," in addition to the two generally recognized ones, the "private sector" of business and the "public sector" of government. It needs an autonomous *social sector.*

PATRIOTISM IS NOT ENOUGH

Patriotism is the willingness to die for one's country. Earlier in this century, the Marxists prophesied that the working class would no longer be patriots; their allegiance would be to their class rather than to their country. This turned out to be a false prophecy. People—and especially working people—are still willing to die for their country, even in the least popular of wars. But patriotism alone is not enough. There has to be citizenship as well.*

Citizenship is the willingness to contribute to one's country. It means the willingness to live—rather than to die—for one's country. To restore citizenship is a central requirement of the post-capitalist polity.

Patriotism, the willingness to die for one's country, has been universal. But citizenship is a distinctly Western invention. It was in effect what Athens and Rome in their glory were all about. And the finest political statement of the Western tradition is about citizenship: the rousing speech which the Greek historian Thucydides put in the mouth of Pericles, the Athenian leader.

---

* "Patriotism is not enough," said the English nurse Edith Cavell during World War I, as she was led to her execution by the Germans for having sheltered escaping British prisoners of war in the Belgian hospital which she ran.

Citizenship disappeared with the collapse of Rome. The Middle Ages did not have citizens: feudal lords had retainers, cities had burghers, the Church had communicants—but no one had citizens. Nor did Japan have citizens before the Meiji Restoration of 1867. The *daimyo*, the lord, had retainers; the urban centers had craft guilds; the religious sects had worshippers. But there were no citizens.

The national state reinvented citizenship, and was in fact built on it. What citizenship means in terms of rights and obligations has ever since been a central issue of political theory and political practice.

As a legal term, "citizenship" is a term of identification rather than of action. As a political term, "citizenship" means active commitment. It means responsibility. It means making a difference in one's community, in one's society, in one's country.

In the Megastate, political citizenship can no longer function. Even if the country is small, the affairs of government are so far away that individuals cannot make a difference. Individuals can vote—and we have learned the hard way these last decades how important the right to vote is. Individuals can pay taxes—and again we have learned the hard way these last decades that this is a meaningful obligation. But the individuals cannot take responsibility, cannot take action to make a difference. Without citizenship, however, the polity is empty. There can be nationalism, but without citizenship, it is likely to degenerate from patriotism into chauvinism. Without citizenship, there cannot be that responsible commitment which creates the citizen and which in the last analysis holds together the body politic. Nor can there be the sense of satisfaction and pride that comes from making a difference. Without citizenship, the political unit, whether called "state" or "empire," can only be a power. Power is then the only thing that holds it together. In order to be able to act in a rapidly changing and dangerous world, the post-capitalist polity must re-create citizenship.

THE NEED FOR COMMUNITY

Equally, there is a need to restore community. Traditional communities no longer have much integrating power; they cannot survive the mobility which knowledge confers on the individual. Traditional communities, we have now learned, were held together far less by what their members had in common than by necessity, if not by coercion and fear.

There is a great deal of talk these days about the disintegration of the family. To some extent, this is misunderstanding. To be sure, a substantial number of marriages in the developed world end in divorce. But marriages are not shorter now than they were a hundred or a hundred and fifty years ago. Then, it was death that dissolved them rather than divorce.

The traditional family was a necessity. In nineteenth-century fiction most families were what we would now call "broken families." But they had to stay together, no matter how great their hatred, their loathing, their fear of each other. "Family is where they have to take you in," was a nineteenth-century saying. Family before this century provided practically all the social services available. To cling to family was a necessity; to be repudiated by it, a catastrophe. A stock figure of American plays and movies as late as the 1920s was the cruel father who threw out his daughter when she came home with an illegitimate child. She then had only two choices: to commit suicide or to become a prostitute.

Today, family is actually becoming more important to most people. But it is becoming so as a voluntary bond, as a bond of affection, of attachment, of mutual respect, rather than one of necessity. Today's young people, once they have grown out of adolescent rebellion, feel a much greater need than my generation did to be close to their parents and to their siblings.

Still, family no longer makes up the community. But people do need a community. They need it particularly in the sprawling huge cities and suburbs in which more and more of us live. One can no longer count—as one could in the rural village—on neighbors who share the same interests, the same occupations, the same ignorance, and who live together in the same world. Even if the bond is close, one cannot count on family. Geographic and occupational mobility mean that people no longer stay in the place, class, or culture where they were born, where their parents live, where their siblings and their cousins live. The community that is needed in post-capitalist society—and needed especially by the knowledge worker—has to be based on *commitment and compassion* rather than being imposed by proximity and isolation.

THE VANISHING PLANT COMMUNITY

Forty years ago, I thought that this community would come into being at the place of work. In *The Future of Industrial Man* (1942), *The New Society* (1949), and *The Practice of Management* (1954), I talked of the plant community as the place that would grant the individual status and function, as well as the responsibility of self-government. But even in Japan, the plant community is not going to work much longer. It is becoming increasingly clear that the Japanese plant community is based far less on a sense of belonging than on fear. A worker in a large Japanese company with its seniority wage system who loses his job past age thirty has become virtually unemployable for the rest of his life. But that too is changing as Japan moves from a serious shortage of jobs—the norm as recently as 1960—to a serious shortage of available labor.

In the West, the plant community never took root. I still strongly maintain that the employee has to be given the maximum responsibility and self-control—the idea that underlay my advocacy of the plant community. The knowledge-based organization has to become a responsibility-based organization.

But individuals, and especially knowledge workers, need an additional sphere of social life, of personal relationships, and of contribution outside and beyond the job, outside and beyond the organization, indeed, outside and beyond their own specialized knowledge area.

174

THE VOLUNTEER AS CITIZEN

The one area in which this need can be satisfied is the social sector. There, individuals can contribute. They can have responsibility. They can make a difference. They can be "volunteers." This is already happening in the United States.

In most other developed countries, the volunteer tradition was crushed by the Welfare State. In Japan, for instance, temples and Shinto shrines were active centers of community service with strong participation by local volunteers. The 1867 Meiji Restoration "Westernized" by making religion into a government function—and both the volunteers and the temple community services soon disappeared. In Britain, all through the nineteenth century charity was a community activity and seen as a responsibility of the well-to-do. After 1890, with the growing belief in government as the master of society, most of this disappeared. The Salvation Army (founded in London in 1878) is one of the few survivors of what was a flourishing culture of community service in Victorian times. And in France, *any* community action that is not organized and controlled by government has been suspect since Napoleon, and is in fact considered almost subversive.

The denominational diversity of American churches; the strong emphasis on local autonomy of states, counties, cities; and the community tradition of isolated frontier settlements all slowed down the politization and centralization of social activities in the United States. As a result, America now has almost one million non-profit organizations active in the social sector. They represent as much as one tenth of the gross national product—one quarter of that sum raised by donations from the public, another quarter paid by government for specific work (e.g., to administer health care reimbursement programs), the rest fees for services rendered (e.g., tuition paid by students attending private universities or money made by the art stores to be found now in every American museum).

The non-profits have become America's biggest employer.

Every other American adult (90 million people all told) works at least three hours a week as "unpaid staff," that is, as a volunteer for a non-profit organization, for churches and hospitals, for health care agencies, for community services like the Red Cross, Boy Scouts, and Girl Scouts, for rehabilitation services like the Salvation Army and Alcoholics Anonymous, for shelters for battered wives, and for tutoring services in inner-city schools. By the year 2000 or 2010, the number of such unpaid staff people should have risen to 120 million, and their average hours of work to five per week.

These volunteers are no longer "helpers"; they have become "partners." Non-profit organizations in the United States increasingly have a full-time paid executive, but the rest of the management team are volunteers. Increasingly, they run the organization.

The greatest change has taken place in the American Catholic Church. In one major diocese, lay women now actually run all the parishes as "parish administrators." The priests say Mass and dispense the sacraments. Everything else, including all the social and community work of the parishes, is done by "unpaid staff," led by the parish administrator.

The main reason for this upsurge of volunteer participation in the United States is not an increase in need. The main reason is the search on the part of the volunteers for community, for commitment, for contribution. The great bulk of the new volunteers are not retired people; they are husbands and wives in the professional, two-earner family, people in their thirties and forties, well educated, affluent, busy. They enjoy their jobs. But they feel the need to do something where "we can make a difference," to use the phrase one hears again and again—whether that means running a Bible class in the local church; teaching disadvantaged children the multiplication tables; or visiting old people back home from a long stay in the hospital and helping them with their rehabilitation exercises.

What the U.S. non-profits do for their volunteers may well be just as important as what they do for the recipients of their services.

The Girl Scouts of America is one of the few American organizations that has become racially integrated. In their troops, girls regardless of color or national origin work together and play together. But the greatest contribution of the integration drive which the Girl Scouts began in the 1970s, is that it recruited a large number of mothers—black, Asian, Hispanic—into leadership positions as volunteers in integrated community work.

Similarly, the greatest attraction of the American "pastoral" churches is the effective community activity they offer their volunteers. These churches are almost totally volunteer-staffed. One of the largest of them has 13,000 members but only 150 paid staff people, including the senior pastor. Yet it does more community work than any traditional church has ever done. Everyone who joins the congregation is expected, after attending for a few Sundays, to start working for a church activity—either in the church itself or in the outside community. A few months later, he or she will then be asked to take over the management of such an activity. Everybody is expected to be a "leader."

Citizenship in and through the social sector is not a panacea for the ills of post-capitalist society and post-capitalist polity, but it may be a prerequisite for tackling these ills. It restores the civic responsibility that is the mark of citizenship, and the civic pride that is the mark of community.

The need is greatest where community and community organizations—and citizenship altogether—have been so thoroughly damaged as to have been almost totally destroyed: in the ex-Communist countries. Government in these countries has not only been totally discredited; it has become totally impotent. It may take years before the successor governments to the Communists—in Czechoslovakia and Kazakhstan, in Russia, Poland, the Ukraine—can competently carry out the tasks which only government can do: managing money and taxes; running the military and the courts; conducting foreign relations. In the meantime, only autonomous, local non-profits—organizations of the social sector based on volunteers and releasing the spiritual energies of people—can provide both the social services that the society needs and the leadership development that the polity needs.

Different societies and different countries will surely struc-ture the social sector very differently. In Western Europe, for instance, the churches are unlikely to play the key role that they play in a still largely Christian America. In Japan, membership in the employee community may well remain the central focus and badge of community, especially for rank-and-file workers. But every developed country needs an autonomous, self-governing social sector of community organizations—to provide the requi-site community services, but above all to restore the bonds of community and a sense of active citizenship. Historically, commu-nity was fate. In the post-capitalist society and polity, community has to become commitment.

PART THREE

KNOWLEDGE

10

Knowledge: Its Economics and Its Productivity

A T FIRST GLANCE, the economy appears hardly to have been affected by the shift to knowledge as the basic resource. It seems to have remained "capitalist" rather than "post-capitalist." But looks are deceptive.

The economy will, to be sure, remain a market economy—and a worldwide one. It will reach even further than did the world market economy before World War I, when there were no "planned" economies and no "Socialist" countries. Criticism of the market as the organizer of economic activity goes back all the way to Aristotle. Most of the charges against it are well founded.* But as no less an anti-capitalist than Karl Marx pointed out more than a hundred years ago, the market, for all its imperfections, is still vastly superior to all other ways of organizing economic activity—something that the last forty years have amply proven. What makes the market superior is precisely that it organizes economic activity around *information*.

* Among the most cogent of such criticisms is that of Karl Polanyi (1886–1964) in his *The Great Transformation* (1944).

But while the world economy will remain a market economy and retain the market institutions, its substance has been radically changed. If it is still "capitalist," it is now dominated by "information capitalism." The industries that have moved into the center of the economy in the last forty years have as their business the production and distribution of knowledge and information, rather than the production and distribution of things. The actual product of the pharmaceutical industry is knowledge; pill and prescription ointment are no more than packaging for knowledge. There are the telecommunications industries and the industries which produce information-processing tools and equipment, such as computers, semiconductors, software. There are the information producers and distributors: movies, television shows, videocassettes. The "non-businesses" which produce and apply knowledge—education and health care—have in all developed countries grown much faster even than knowledge-based businesses.

The "super-rich" of the old capitalism were the nineteenth-century steel barons. The "super-rich" of the post–World War II boom are computer makers, software makers, producers of television shows, and Ross Perot, the builder of a business installing and running information systems. Such great fortunes as were made in retailing—those of Sam Walton of Wal-Mart in the United States, Masatoshi Ito of Ito-Yokado in Japan, or the Sainsbury brothers in the United Kingdom—were made by reorganizing this old business around information.

In fact, whichever traditional industries managed to grow during the past forty years did so because they restructured themselves around knowledge and information. The integrated steel mill is becoming obsolete; even in low-wage countries, as we have seen, it cannot compete against the minimill. But a minimill is simply a steelmaker organized around information rather than around heat.

It is no longer possible to make huge profits on doing or moving things. It is no longer even possible to make huge profits by controlling money.

In 1910, an Austro-German Socialist, Rudolf Hilferding (1877–1941), coined the term "Finance Capitalism." He asserted that this was the ultimate stage of Capitalism before the inevitable coming of Socialism. In a capitalist economy, he postulated, the margin between what banks pay for money and what is being charged for it widens inexorably. As a result, banks and bankers become the only profit makers and the rulers of capitalist economy. Lenin, a few years later, made this thesis the basis of his theory of Communism. This explains why Soviet planning was organized around the State Bank and controlled through the allocation of bank credit. Finance Capitalism was still Socialist dogma after World War II, which explains why the post-war Labour government in Great Britain immediately nationalized the Bank of England, and why, a few years later, the first Socialist government in France nationalized the main commercial banks.

Today, commercial banks are everywhere in trouble. The margin between what they pay for money and what they get for it is shrinking steadily. They cannot make a good living by earning a return on money. Increasingly, they can only make a living—let alone a profit—by receiving fees for information.

Increasingly, there is less and less return on the traditional resources: labor, land and (money) capital. The main producers of wealth have become information and knowledge.

THE ECONOMICS OF KNOWLEDGE

How knowledge behaves as an *economic* resource, we do not yet fully understand; we have not had enough experience to formulate a theory and to test it. We can only say so far that we need such a theory. We need an economic theory that puts knowledge into the center of the wealth-producing process. Such a theory alone can explain the present economy. It alone can explain economic growth. It alone can explain innovation. It alone can explain how the Japanese economy works and, above all, why it works. It alone can explain why newcomers, especially in high-tech fields, can, almost overnight, sweep the market and drive out all competitors, no matter how well entrenched they are—as the Japanese did in consumer electronics and in the U.S. automobile market.

So far, there are no signs of an Adam Smith or a David Ricardo of knowledge. But the first studies of the economic behavior of knowledge have begun to appear.*

These studies make clear that the knowledge-based economy does not behave the way existing theory assumes an economy to behave. We therefore know that the new economic theory, the theory of a knowledge-based economy, will be quite different from any existing economic theory, whether Keynesian or Neo-Keynesian, classical or neo-classical.

One of the economists' basic assumptions is that "perfect competition" is the model for the allocation of resources but also for the distribution of economic rewards. Imperfect competition is common in the "real world." But it is assumed to be the result of outside interference with the economy, i.e., of monopoly; of patent protection; of government regulation; and so on. But in the knowledge economy, imperfect competition seems to be inherent in the economy itself. Initial advantages gained through early application and exploitation of knowledge (that is, through what has come to be known as the "learning curve") become permanent and irreversible. What this implies is that neither free trade economics nor protectionism will by themselves work as economic policies. The knowledge economy seems to require both in balance.

Another of the economists' basic assumptions is that an economy is determined either by consumption or by investment.

* Examples are the work done by Paul Romer of the University of California, Berkeley, such as his two articles "Endogenous Technical Change," in the *Journal of Political Economy* (1990), and "Are Nonconvexities Important for Understanding Growth?" in *American Economic Review* (1990); the work done by Maurice Scott of Oxford, especially his book *A New View of Economic Growth* (Oxford University Press, 1989); and the article by Jacob T. Schwartz, a New York University mathematician and computer scientist, "America's Economic-Technological Agenda for the 1990s," in *Daedalus*, the Journal of the American Academy of Arts and Sciences (Winter 1992)—the last a rigorous yet jargon-free presentation of the economics of knowledge-based innovation.

Keynesians and Neo-Keynesians (such as Milton Friedman) make it dependent on consumption; classicists and neo-classicists (those of the Austrian School) on investment. In the knowledge economy, neither seems to be in control. There is no shred of evidence that increased *consumption* in the economy leads to greater production of knowledge. But there is also no shred of evidence that greater *investment* in the economy leads to greater production of knowledge. At least the lead times between increased consumption and knowledge production, or between increased investment and knowledge production, seem to be so long as to defy analysis—and surely too long to base either economic theory or economic policy on the correlation, whatever it might be.

Equally incompatible with traditional economic theory is the absence of a common denominator for different kinds of knowledge. Different pieces of land give different yields; but their price is determined by these differences, that is, by quantity of output. When it comes to new knowledge, there are three kinds (as already discussed in Chapter 4 above). There is first the continuing *improvement* of process, product, service; the Japanese, who do it best, call this *Kaizen.* Then there is *exploitation*: the continuous exploitation of existing knowledge to develop new and different products, processes, and services. Finally, there is genuine *innovation.*

These three ways of applying knowledge to produce change in the economy (and in society as well) need to be worked at together and at the same time. They are all equally necessary. But their economic characteristics—their costs as well as their economic impacts—are qualitatively different. So far, at least, it is not possible to *quantify* knowledge. We can, of course, estimate how much it costs to produce and distribute knowledge. But how much is produced—indeed, what we might even mean by "return on knowledge"—we cannot say. Yet we can have no economic theory unless there is a model that expresses economic events in quantitative relationships. Without it, there is no way to make a rational choice—and rational choices are what economics is all about.

Above all, the *amount* of knowledge, that is, its quantitative aspect, is not nearly as important as the *productivity* of knowledge, that is, its qualitative impact. And this applies to old knowledge and its application, as well as to new knowledge.

THE PRODUCTIVITY OF KNOWLEDGE

Knowledge does not come cheap. All developed countries spend something like a fifth of their GNP on the production and dissemination of knowledge. Formal schooling—schooling of young people before they enter the labor force—takes up about one tenth of GNP (up from 2 percent or so at the time of World War I). Employing organizations spend another 5 percent of GNP on the continuing education of their employees; it may be more. And 3 to 5 percent of GNP is spent on research and development—on the production of new knowledge.

Very few countries set aside a similar portion of their GNP to form traditional, that is money, capital. Even in Japan and Germany, the two major countries with the highest rates of capital formation, the rate exceeded one fifth of GNP only during the forty years of most feverish rebuilding and expansion in the post–World War II period. In the United States, capital formation has not reached 20 percent of GNP for many years.

Knowledge formation is thus already the largest investment in every developed country. Surely, the return which a country or a company gets on knowledge must increasingly be a determining factor in its competitiveness. Increasingly, productivity of knowledge will be decisive in its economic and social success, and in its entire economic performance. And we know that there are tremendous differences in the productivity of knowledge—between countries, between industries, between individual organizations.

Here are a few examples:

According to its production of scientific and technical knowledge, Great Britain should have been the world's economic leader in the post–World War II era. Antibiotics, the jet plane, the body scanner, even the computer were all British developments. But Britain did not succeed in turning these knowledge achievements into successful products and services, into jobs, into exports, into market standing. The lack of productivity of its knowledge, more than anything else, is at the root of the slow and steady erosion of the British economy.

Similar danger signs abound today with respect to the productivity of knowledge in American society. In industry after industry—from microchips to fax machines and from machine tools to copiers—American companies have generated the new technologies, only to see Japanese companies develop the products and take over the markets. In the United States, the additional output for each additional input of knowledge is clearly lower than that of its Japanese competitors. In important areas, the productivity of knowledge in the United States is falling behind.

Germany furnishes a different example. Post–World War II Germany—at least until 1990 and reunification—recorded an impressive economic achievement. In most industries, but also in such areas as banking and insurance, West Germany attained stronger leadership positions than were held by either Imperial or pre-Hitler Germany. West Germany, year after year, exported four times as much per capita as the United States and three times as much as Japan. West Germany thus showed an exceedingly high productivity in old knowledge—in applying it, improving it, exploiting it. But it showed an extremely low productivity in new knowledge, and especially in the new "high-tech" areas: computers, telecommunications, pharmaceuticals, advanced materials, biogenetics, and so on. Proportionately, West Germany invested as much money and talent in these areas as did the United States—maybe more. It produced a fair amount of new knowledge. But it has signally failed to convert that new knowledge into successful innovation. The new knowledge has remained information rather than become productive.

The most instructive example is Japan. Japan has done particularly well these last forty years both in traditional manufacturing and in new knowledge-based industries. Yet Japan's meteoric rise was not based on *producing* knowledge. In technology and in management, most of Japan's knowledge was produced elsewhere, the bulk of it in the United States. Serious work in Japan on building a knowledge base at home hardly even began until the late 1970s; and even now, when it has long been the world's number-two economic power, Japan still imports more knowledge than it exports. At that, the Japanese did not actually import a very great deal of technological (as distinct from management) knowledge. But they made superbly productive use of whatever knowledge they acquired.

It is likely that the productivity of resources will altogether become a central concern of economics in the post-capitalist society. It underlies the relationship between environment and economic growth. That this new concern will lead to very different economies is one of the consequences of our recent work on the productivity of money.

THE PRODUCTIVITY OF MONEY

The productivity of money was ignored by economists until World War II. Practically all of them, including Marx, thought in terms of the quantity of capital rather than in terms of its productivity. Even Keynes distinguished only between money invested and money hoarded. He took for granted the productivity of money once it had been invested.

But in the post–World War II years, we began to ask: How much added production does an additional unit of invested money generate? What is the productivity of capital? It then became apparent that there are differences in the productivity of money capital, and that these differences matter greatly.

At the time when concern with productivity of capital first arose—in the late 1950s and early 1960s—central planning was all the rage worldwide. People were concerned only as to whether the detailed top-down planning by command of the Soviet Five Year Plans or the consensus planning of the French *Plan Indicatif* was the better way to run the economy. Almost everybody accepted that the results which planning yielded were vastly superior to the unplanned capital allocation of the market, both in total output and in output per unit of investment.

The very first attempts to measure actual performance showed conclusively that under both types of planning, the productivity of capital is very low and is declining steadily. They showed that under central planning, additional units of capital investment yield less and less additional output.

The French immediately acted. They shelved the *Plan Indicatif*, and with it economic planning. If France had not thus changed course by 180 degrees in the early sixties, it would today look very much the way East Germany does.

The Soviet planners kept on planning. And the productivity of capital in the Soviet Empire kept on falling—to the point where it actually became negative. In the Brezhnev years, agricultural investment rose steadily until it took the lion's share of all available non-defense money. But the more money the Soviets poured into farming, the smaller their harvests became. And the same negative productivity of capital also engulfed civilian industries in the USSR (we have no information on what happened in the defense sector). It was the failure of the productivity of capital, more than anything else, that brought about the collapse of the Soviet economy in the end.

Centralization, we now know, seriously impedes the productivity of money capital. The tremendous investments in the Third World made by the World Bank were not centrally planned. But they were—and are—highly centralized. Their productivity has been low. They have built highly visible monuments such as enormous steel mills; but they have had very few "multiplier" effects on the whole. They have created few jobs outside the plant gates. They have rarely become economically self-sustaining, let alone profitable. Thus, they act as a drag on the national economy, rather than supplying it with additional investment capital.

It is highly likely that centralized planning and indeed centralization in general will make knowledge capital as unproductive as it does money capital.

Japanese planning for "high-tech" knowledge is as much the rage these days as Russian and French planning for economic development was about thirty years ago. Yet the results so far are singularly unimpressive. The Japanese triumphs in high-tech industries owe very little to the much-touted government plans. Most of them have been failures (e.g., the ambitious plan to develop the "Fifth-Generation" supercomputer). And the various U.S. plans to beat the Japanese through government-sponsored "consortia," that is, through centralization of innovation, have also been quite unsuccessful.

Innovation, that is, the application of knowledge to produce new knowledge, is not, as so much American folklore asserts, "inspiration" and best done by loners in their garages. It requires systematic effort, and a high degree of organization.* But it also requires both decentralization and diversity, that is, the opposite of central planning and centralization.

THE MANAGEMENT REQUIREMENTS

"Centralization," "decentralization," and "diversity" are not terms of economics. They are management terms. We do not have an economic theory of the productivity of knowledge investment; we may never have one. But we have *management precepts*. We know above all that making knowledge productive is a management responsibility. It cannot be discharged by government; but it also cannot be done by market forces. It requires systematic, organized application of knowledge to knowledge.

The first rule may well be that knowledge has to aim high to produce results. The steps may be small and incremental but the goal must be ambitious. Knowledge is productive only if it is applied to make a difference.

The Hungarian-American Nobel prizewinner Albert Szent-Györgyi (1893–1990) revolutionized physiology. When asked to

* On this see my 1986 book *Innovation and Entrepreneurship* (New York: Harper & Row; London: Wm. Heinemann).

190

explain his achievements, he gave the credit to his teacher, an otherwise obscure professor at a provincial Hungarian university. "When I got my doctorate," Szent-Györgyi said, "I proposed to study flatulence—nothing was known about it and nothing is known about it still." "Very interesting," the professor said, "but no one has ever died of flatulence. If you have results (and it's a big 'if'), you'd better have them where they'll make a difference." "And so," Szent-Györgyi went on, "I took up the study of basic bodily chemistry and discovered the enzymes."

Every single one of Szent-Györgyi's research projects was a small step. But from the beginning he aimed high: discovery of the basic chemistry of the human body. Similarly, in Japanese *Kaizen*, every single step is a small one—a minor change here, a minor improvement there. But the aim is to produce by means of step-by-step improvements a radically different product, process, or service a few years later. The aim is *to make a difference*.

To make knowledge productive further requires that it be clearly focused. It has to be highly concentrated. Whether done by an individual or by a team, the knowledge effort requires purpose and organization. It is not "flash of genius." It is hard work.

To make knowledge productive also requires the systematic exploitation of opportunities for change—what in an earlier book I called the "Seven Windows of Innovation."* These opportunities have to be matched with the competences and strengths of the knowledge worker and the knowledge team.

To make knowledge productive finally requires managing time. High knowledge productivity—whether in improvement, in exploitation, or in innovation—comes at the end of a long gestation period. Yet productivity of knowledge also requires a constant stream of short-term results. It thus requires the most difficult of all management achievements: balancing the long term with the short term.

Our experience in making knowledge productive has so far been gained mainly in the economy and technology. But the same

* *Innovation and Entrepreneurship.*

rules pertain to making knowledge productive in society, in the polity, and with respect to knowledge itself. So far, little work has been done to apply knowledge to these areas. But we need productivity of knowledge even more in these areas than we need it in the economy, in technology, or in medicine.

ONLY CONNECT . . .

The productivity of knowledge requires increasing the yield from what is known—whether by the individual or by the group. There is an old American story of the farmer who turns down a proposal for a more productive farming method by saying, "I already know how to farm twice as well as I do."

Most of us (perhaps all of us) know many times more than we put to use. The main reason is that we do not mobilize the multiple knowledges we possess. We do not use knowledges as part of one toolbox. Instead of asking: "What do I know, what have I learned, that might apply to this task?" we tend to classify tasks in terms of specialized knowledge areas.

Again and again in working with executives I find that a given challenge in organizational structure, for instance, or in technology yields to knowledge the executives already possess: They may have acquired it, for instance, in an economics course at the university. "Of course, I know that," is the standard response, "but it's economics, not management." This is a purely arbitrary distinction—necessary perhaps to learn and to teach a "subject," but irrelevant as a definition of what knowledge is and what it can do. The way we traditionally arrange our businesses, government agencies, and universities further encourages the tendency to believe that the purpose of the tools is to adorn the toolbox rather than to do work.

In learning and teaching, we do have to focus on the tool. In usage, we have to focus on the end result, on the task, on the work. "Only connect" was the constant admonition of a great English novelist, E. M. Forster. It has always been the hallmark of the artist, but equally of the great scientist—of a Darwin, a Bohr, an

Einstein. At their level, the capacity to connect may be inborn and part of that mystery we call "genius." But to a large extent, the ability to connect and thus to raise the yield of existing knowledge (whether for an individual, for a team, or for the entire organization) is learnable. Eventually, it should become teachable. It requires a methodology for *problem definition*—even more urgently perhaps than it requires the currently fashionable methodology for "problem solving." It requires systematic analysis of the kind of knowledge and information a given problem requires, and a methodology for organizing the stages in which a given problem can be tackled—the methodology which underlies what we now call "systems research." It requires what might be called "Organizing Ignorance"*—and there is always so much more ignorance around than there is knowledge.

Specialization into knowledges has given us enormous performance potential in each area. But because knowledges are so specialized, we need also a methodology, a discipline, a process to turn this potential into performance. Otherwise, most of the available knowledge will not become productive; it will remain mere information.

Not to see the forest for the trees is a serious failing. But it is an equally serious failing not to see the trees for the forest. One can only plant and cut down individual trees. Yet the forest is the "ecology," the environment without which individual trees would never grow. To make knowledge productive, we will have to learn to see both forest and tree. We will have to learn to connect.

The productivity of knowledge is going to be the determining factor in the competitive position of a company, an industry, an entire country. No country, industry, or company has any "natural" advantage or disadvantage. The only advantage it can possess is the ability to exploit universally available knowledge. The only thing that increasingly will matter in national as in international economics is management's performance in making knowledge productive.

* The title of a book I began to write forty years ago but never finished.

11

The Accountable School

A TECHNOLOGICAL REVOLUTION—desktop computers and satellite transmission directly into the classroom—is engulfing our schools. It will transform the way we learn and the way we teach within a few decades. It will change the economics of education. From being almost totally labor-intensive, schools will become highly capital-intensive.

But more drastic still—though rarely discussed as yet—will be the changes in the social position and role of the school. Though long a central institution, it has been "of society" rather than "in society." It concerned itself with the young, who were not yet citizens, not yet responsible, not yet in the work force. In the knowledge society, the school becomes the institution of the adults as well, and especially of highly schooled adults. Above all, in the knowledge society, the school becomes accountable for performance and results.

In the West, the school underwent an earlier technological revolution several hundred years ago, brought about by the printed book. This earlier revolution holds important lessons for today—and lessons that are not technological. One lesson: that embracing the new technology of learning and teaching is a prerequisite for national and cultural success—and equally for economic competitiveness.

The West moved into leadership throughout the world between 1500 and 1650 in large measure because it reorganized its schools around the new technology of the printed book. Conversely, the refusal of China and Islam to redesign their schools around the printed book was a major factor in their decline and their eventually succumbing to the West. Both used printing—the Chinese had done so for centuries, of course (albeit not with movable type). But both kept the printed book out of their schools; both rejected it as a learning and teaching tool. The Islamic clergy stuck to rote learning and recitation; they saw in the printed book a threat to their authority precisely because it enabled students to read on their own. In China, too, the Confucian scholars rejected the printed book in favor of calligraphy. The printed book was incompatible with a key tenet of Chinese culture: mastery of calligraphy qualifies for rulership.

Before 1550, China and the Ottoman Empire—the political embodiment of Islam—were the world's "superpowers" in every arena: politically, militarily, economically, scientifically, and culturally. Until 1550, both were in the ascendant. From 1550 on, both became increasingly stagnant. Both became inward-looking; both went on the defensive. In the West, the school came to be seen as the "progressive" institution and as the engine of advance in all areas—in culture, the arts, in literature and science, in the economy, politics, and the military. In Islam and in China, by contrast, the school came increasingly to be seen as a major obstacle to progress; rebellion against the school was the starting point for all reform movements in these two great civilizations.

The earlier revolution in learning demonstrates a second, equally important lesson: technology itself matters less than the changes which it triggers in substance, content, and focus of schooling and school. These changes in substance, content, and focus are what really matter. They are effective even if there is only a minimum of change in the technology of learning and teaching.

HOW THE JAPANESE DID IT

This is what Japan demonstrates. The Japanese followed neither the Western model in their "new" and "modern" schools—the schools which the *bunjin* (i.e., literati, or humanist) movement of the Kyoto Renaissance developed in the late eighteenth and early nineteenth centuries. Japan did not put the printed book at the center; in fact, Japanese calligraphy reached its peak in the schools the *bunjin* founded in Kyoto, which then spread throughout the entire country. Their schools stressed the discipline calligraphy imparts and the aesthetic perception it trains—as does Japanese education to this day. The schools of the *bunjin* did not, however, shun the printed book as the Chinese had done. They used it very effectively. Above all, they rejected the Chinese idea of the "scholar" as an elite group, separate and different from ordinary folk. The *bunjin* aimed at universal literacy; wherever they went, they induced the local lord to start schools for the children in his domain, open to all. And in content and substance the *bunjin* school drew heavily on everything it could learn from the West and Western education—mostly through the Dutch traders who resided in Nagasaki. In fact, these schools of the Kyoto Renaissance two hundred years ago are perhaps the best example of that unique Japanese faculty to absorb foreign culture—in this case, both Chinese and Western culture—and to "Japanize" it.

It was the *bunjin* school which, a century later, enabled the Japanese, alone among non-Western peoples, to become a modern nation, to become "Westernized" in its economy, technology, political institutions, and the military, and yet still to remain profoundly Japanese. Every one of the men who in the late nineteenth century transformed the isolated and still feudal Japan of the Tokugawa Shogunate into the "modern" Japan of the Meiji

Restoration had been a student in a *bunjin* school taught by one of the great *bunjin* masters or their disciples.

Technology, however important and however visible, will not be the most important feature of the transformation in education. Most important will be rethinking the role and function of schooling—its focus, its purpose, its values. The technology will still be significant, but primarily because it should force us to do new things rather than because it will enable us to do old things better.

Again, the earlier European revolution in learning and teaching furnishes an example. The greatest figure of this development, the one man who can be called the "father of the modern school," was John Ámos Comenius (1592–1670), a Czech Protestant (his original name was Komenský) driven out of his homeland by the Catholic counter-reformation that followed the defeat of the Czech uprising in 1618 against the Catholic Hapsburgs. We owe to Comenius the technology that made the printed book the effective carrier of learning and teaching; he invented the primer and the textbook. But these were to him only tools. His school centered on a new curriculum. It is still, by and large, what schools throughout the world consider "education." His aim was universal literacy. And his motivation was religious: to enable his Czech compatriots to remain Protestants and to read and study the Bible on their own, even though their religion had been suppressed and their pastors driven out by the victorious Papists.

The real challenge ahead is thus not the technology itself. It is what we use it for. So far, no country has the educational system which the knowledge society needs. No country has tackled the major demands. No one knows "the answers"; no one can do what is needed. But we can at least ask the questions. We can define—albeit in rough outline—the specifications for schooling and for schools which might answer to the realities of the post-capitalist society, the knowledge society.

These specifications call for a school as different from the one that exists now as the "modern" school for which Comenius drew up the specifications three hundred and fifty years ago differed from the school that existed before the printed book.

Here are the new specifications:

- The school we need has to provide universal literacy of a high order—well beyond what "literacy" means today.

- It has to imbue students on all levels and of all ages with motivation to learn and with the discipline of continuing learning.

- It has to be an open system, accessible both to highly educated people and to people who for whatever reason did not gain access to advanced education in their early years.

- It has to impart knowledge both as substance and as process—what the Germans differentiate as *Wissen* and *Können.*

- Finally, schooling can no longer be a monopoly of the schools. Education in the post-capitalist society has to permeate the entire society. Employing organizations of all kinds—businesses, government agencies, non-profits—must become institutions of learning and teaching as well. Schools, increasingly, must work in partnership with employers and employing organizations.

THE NEW PERFORMANCE DEMANDS

Universal literacy of a very high order is the first priority. It is the foundation. Without it, no society can hope to be capable of high performance in the post-capitalist world and in its knowledge society. To equip individual students with the tools to perform, to contribute, and to be employable is also the first social duty of any educational system.

The new technology of learning will have its first impact on universal literacy. Most schools throughout the ages have spent endless hours trying to teach things that are best learned rather than taught, that is, things that are being learned behaviorally and through drill, repetition, feedback. Here belong most of the subjects taught in elementary school, but also a good many of the subjects taught in later stages of the educational process. Such subjects—whether reading and writing, arithmetic, spelling, historical facts, biology, and even such advanced subjects as neurosurgery, medical diagnosis, and most of engineering—are best learned through a computer program. The teacher motivates, directs, encourages. The teacher, in fact, becomes a leader and a resource.

In the school of tomorrow the students will be their own instructors, with a computer program as their own tool. Indeed, the younger the students are, the more the computer appeals to them, the more successfully it guides and instructs them. Historically, the elementary school has been totally labor-intensive. Tomorrow's elementary school will be heavily capital-intensive.

Yet, despite the available technology, universal literacy poses tremendous challenges. The traditional concepts of literacy no longer suffice. Reading, writing, arithmetic will be needed just as they are today, but literacy now has to go well beyond these foundations. It requires numeracy; it requires a basic understanding of science and of the dynamics of technology; it requires an acquaintance with foreign languages. It also requires learning how to be effective as a member of an organization, as an employee.

Universal literacy implies a clear commitment to the priority of schooling. It demands that the school—especially the school of the beginners, the children—subordinate everything else to the acquisition of foundation skills. Unless the school successfully imparts these skills to the young learner, it has failed in its crucial duty: to give beginners self-confidence, to give them competence, and to make them capable, a few years hence, to perform and achieve in the post-capitalist society, the knowledge society.

This requires a reversal of the prevailing trend in modern education and especially in American education. Having, as we thought, achieved universal literacy by the end of World War I or, at the latest, by the end of World War II, American education reversed its priorities. Instead of putting being a learning agency first, it put being a social agency first. In the 1950s and 1960s, when we in the United States made this decision, it was probably an inevitable one. The severity and extent of the racial problem we faced forced us to make the school the agent of racial integration; the legacy of the sin of slavery has been the central American challenge for a hundred and fifty years and is likely to remain the central American challenge for at least another fifty or hundred years.

But the schools could not do this social job. Like every other organization, the schools are good only at their own special-purpose task. Subordinating learning to social goals may have actually impeded racial integration and the advancement of African-American people—as more and more achieving blacks now assert. Yet putting social ends ahead of the goal of learning became a major factor in the decline of American basic education. Upper- and middle-class children still acquire traditional literacy, but the ones who need it most—the children of the poor, especially of poor blacks, and the children of immigrants—do not.

What we have to do now is to reassert the original purpose of the school. It is not social reform or social amelioration; it has to be individual learning. The most hopeful developments in U.S. education may well be that this is increasingly being asserted by achieving African-Americans and Hispanics themselves, such as the black woman legislator in Milwaukee, Wisconsin, who pushed through a "voucher plan" against the strident opposition of the educational establishment. This plan enables parents to choose for their child a school which focuses on, indeed demands, learning.

This will be attacked by liberals and progressives as an elitist position. But the most elitist school, the Japanese school, has created the most egalitarian society. Even those who do not shine in the intensely competitive educational race in Japan still acquire what by any traditional standard is extremely high literacy and an extremely high ability to achieve and perform in modern society. Yet in the Japanese school, literacy is put first, and everything else is subordinated to it. But there are also enough American schools around by now in which the most disadvantaged children learn *because it is expected of them and demanded of them.*

LEARNING TO LEARN

"Literacy" traditionally meant subject knowledge, for example, the ability to do multiplication or a little knowledge of American history. But the knowledge society equally needs *process knowledge*—something the schools have rarely even tried to teach.

In the knowledge society, people have to learn how to learn. Indeed, in the knowledge society, subjects may matter less than the students' capacity to continue learning and their motivation to do so. Post-capitalist society requires lifelong learning. For this, we need a discipline of learning. But lifelong learning also requires that learning be alluring; indeed, that it become a high satisfaction in itself, if not something the individual craves.

Of all educational systems today, only the Japanese try to equip their students with a discipline for learning. The Japanese student who tests so high on a math test at eighteen, ten years later remembers no more math than the American twenty-eight-year-old who tested so abysmally low fifteen years earlier. But the Japanese come out of their schools having learned how to study, how to persist, how to learn.

Yet the Japanese discipline of learning—the discipline of the "examination hell" of the university entrance exam—does not motivate. Based on fear and pressure, it quenches the desire to keep on learning. And it is this desire that we need.

In America's liberal arts colleges, by contrast, learning is enjoyable for many students. But it is enjoyment alone, bereft of discipline. It mistakes "feeling good" for achievement and "being stimulated" for discipline.

Actually, we *do* know what to do. In fact, for hundreds, if not thousands, of years we have been creating both the motivation for continuing learning and the needed discipline. The good teachers of artists do it; the good coaches of athletes do it; so do the good "mentors" in the business organizations of which we hear so much these days in the literature of management development. They lead their students to achievements so great that it surprises the achiever and creates excitement and motivation— especially the motivation for rigorous, disciplined, persistent work and practice which continued learning requires.

> There are few things more boring than practicing scales. Yet the greater and the more accomplished pianists are, the more faithfully do they practice their scales, hour after hour, day after day, week after week. Similarly, the more skilled surgeons are, the more faithfully do they practice tying sutures, hour after hour, day after day, week after week. Pianists do their scales for months on end for an infinitesimally small improvement in technical ability. But this then enables them to achieve the musical result they already hear in their inner ear. Surgeons tie sutures for months on end for an infinitesimally small improvement in their finger dexterity. But this then enables them to speed up an operation and thus save a life. *Achievement is addictive.*

But such achievement does not mean doing a little less poorly what one is not particularly good at. The achievement that motivates is doing exceptionally well what one is already good at. Achievement has to be based on the student's strengths—as has been known for millennia by every teacher of artists, every coach of athletes, every mentor. In fact, finding the student's strengths and focusing them on achievement is the best definition of both teacher and teaching. It is the definition in the "Dialogue on the Teacher" by one of the greatest teachers of the Western tradition, St. Augustine of Hippo (354–430).

Schools and schoolteachers know this too, of course. But they have rarely been allowed to focus on the strengths of students and to challenge them. Instead, they have perforce had to focus on weaknesses. Practically all the time in traditional Western classrooms—at least until graduate school at the university—is spent on remedying weaknesses. It is spent on producing respectable mediocrity.

Students do need to acquire minimal competence in core skills; they do need remedial work; they do need to acquire mediocrity. But in the traditional school, there is practically no time for anything else. The proudest products of the traditional school, "the all-around 'A' students," are the ones who satisfy mediocre standards across the board. They are not the ones who achieve; they are the ones who comply. But, to repeat, the traditional school had no choice. To give every student adequacy in the foundation skills is the first task. This could only be accomplished—even in a small class—by focusing on the weaknesses of students and then remedying them.

Here, the new technologies might make the greatest difference. They free teachers from spending most, if not all, their time on routine learning, remedial learning, repetitive learning. Teachers will still need to lead in these activities. But most of their time has traditionally been spent on "follow-up"; teachers, in an old phrase, spend most of their time being "teaching assistants." And that the computer does well, indeed, better than a human being. Teachers, we can hope, will thus increasingly have the time to identify the strengths of individuals, to focus on them, and to lead students to achievement. They will, we can expect, have the time to *teach*.

But even if technology enables them to do this, will the school change its attitude and focus on strengths? Will it be willing to teach "individuals" rather than "students"? School and teacher will still have to say: "Betsy (or John), you need to do more practice on long division; here are the examples for you to work through." School and teacher will still have to check that Betsy or John then actually does the work. They will still have to sit down with the pupil to explain, demonstrate, and encourage. But with the computer as the teaching assistant, teachers will not have to sit down and supervise the actual work—which is where they now spend most of their time. Will they then be willing to focus on the learner's strengths? Will they be willing to say: "Betsy, you draw so well; why don't you draw pictures of all the kids in the class?"

* * *

There is a second process knowledge to be taught by the schools—or at least learned in them: the process needed to obtain what in the last chapter I called the "yield" from knowledge. The place to accomplish this will probably be in practice rather than in school. The only educational institutions that are so far concerned with the yield from knowledge are "professional" schools, for example, engineering schools, schools of medicine, law schools, management schools. These are the very schools which focus on practice rather than on theory. But everyone will have to be able to raise the yield from knowledge. This requires that the process—the concepts, the diagnosis, the skills—will have to be made teachable, or at least learnable. This is surely an educational challenge.

THE SCHOOL IN SOCIETY

The school has been a central social institution for a long time—in the West at least since the Renaissance, even longer in the Orient. But it has traditionally been "of society" rather than "in society." It has been a separate institution that rarely, if ever, combined with any other institution. The earliest schools in the West, the Benedictine monasteries of the early Middle Ages, primarily trained future monks rather than the laity. And the school was not for grown people; the root of the word "pedagogy"—*paidos*—is the Greek word for "boy."

That the school will now increasingly be *in* society may therefore be as radical a change as any change in teaching and learning methods, in subject matter, or in the teaching and learning process. School will continue to teach the young. But with learning becoming a lifelong activity rather than something one stops upon becoming "grown-up," schools will have to be organized for lifelong learning. Schools will have to become "open systems."

Schools almost everywhere are organized on the assumption that a student has to enter every stage at a given age, with a prescribed and standardized preparation. One starts kindergarten at age five, elementary school at age six, middle school at age twelve, high school at age fifteen, college or university at age eighteen, and so on. If one misses one of these steps (except kindergarten), one is forever out of step and rarely permitted back in.

For the traditional school, this is a self-evident axiom, almost a law of nature. But it is incompatible with the nature of knowledge and with the demands of the knowledge society, the post-capitalist society. What is needed now is a new axiom: "The more schooling a person has, the more often he or she will need further schooling."

In the United States, doctors, lawyers, engineers, business executives are increasingly expected to go back to school every few years lest they become obsolete. Outside of the United States, however, the return of adults to formal schooling is still the exception—and particularly the return of adults to advanced schooling in the very fields in which they have already acquired substantial knowledge and an advanced degree. In Japan, this phenomenon is still almost unknown; but so it is in France, in Italy, and by and large in Germany, Great Britain, and Scandinavia as well. It will have to become standard in all developed countries.

Even more novel is the need to make the educational system open-ended, that is, to allow people to enter its stages at any age. In the United States, this is happening quite fast. And there is England's Open University. But these are only beginnings so far.

The knowledge society can ill afford to waste knowledge potential; and the degree has also become the passport to knowledge jobs. Even in countries like the United States and Japan in which very large numbers of young people go on to the university, many more stop their schooling by the time they are sixteen or eighteen. There is no reason to believe that most of these people lack the intellectual endowment for knowledge work. All our experience proves the opposite. What distinguishes them from the young people who go on to the university is often only lack of money. A fair number of very bright young people do not go on to the university because they are mature at age eighteen and want to be adults rather than continue in the cocoon of adolescence. Ten years later, many want to resume their education. Then—as everyone who has taught them will testify—they become challenging students, if only because of their superior motivation. They now *want* to take on advanced work; the nineteen-year-olds do so because they are *told* to do it.

But even more important: keeping open access to advanced education regardless of age or prior educational credentials is a social necessity. The individual service worker must have the opportunity to move into knowledge work. This in effect means that the post-capitalist society has to create an educational system which, to use a computer term, offers "random access." Individuals must be able at any stage in their lives to continue their formal education and to qualify for knowledge work. Society needs to be willing to accept people into whatever work they are qualified for, regardless of their age.

No society today is organized for this. In fact, most developed countries are organized to keep people in the station in which they begin their working careers. The system is most rigid in Japan, but nearly as rigid in Europe as well. The United States has gone furthest in creating educational opportunities for adults. The growth area in American education these last twenty years has been the continuing education of adults at any age, and the willingness to offer additional, more advanced knowledge in their specialties to already highly educated people. This gives the United States a tremendous advantage over other developed countries. But even in the United States, there is still reluctance to accept people in knowledge work unless they have acquired the basic qualifications fairly early in life.

THE SCHOOLS AS PARTNERS

Schooling will no longer be what schools do. It will increasingly be a joint venture, in which schools are partners rather than monopolists. In many areas, schools will also be only one of several available teaching and learning institutions, in competition with other purveyors of teaching and learning.

School, as has been said before, has traditionally been where you learn; job has been where you work. Increasingly, the line will become blurred. Increasingly, school will be the place where adults continue learning even though they are working full time. They will come back to school for a three-day seminar; for a weekend course; for an intensive three-week stint; or to take courses on two evenings each week for several years until they acquire a degree.

Yet the job will equally be where adults continue learning. Training is of course nothing new, but it used to be restricted to the beginner. Increasingly, training in one form or another will also become lifelong. The adult—and especially the adult with advanced knowledge—will be as much trainer as trainee, as much teacher as student. In the United States, employers already spend almost as much money on training adult employees as the country spends on educating the young in its formal schools.

What is yet to come is a formal partnership between schools and employing institutions. The Germans in their apprenticeship programs have had schools and employers working together for more than a hundred and fifty years training the young. But increasingly schools and employing institutions will have to learn to work together in the advanced education of adults as well. This task—whether the advanced education of highly educated people or makeup education for people who for one reason or another failed to gain access to higher education in the early years—will be carried out in all kinds of partnerships, alliances, internships, in which schools and other organizations work together. The schools need the stimulus of working with adults and employing organizations fully as much as the adults and their employing organizations need the stimulus of working with schools.

THE ACCOUNTABLE SCHOOL

We talk of "good schools" and "poor schools," of "prestige schools" and "also-rans." In Japan, a few universities—Tokyo,

Kyoto, Keio, Waseda, Hitotsubashi—largely control access to careers in major companies and government agencies. In France, the *Grandes Écoles* enjoy a similar position of power and prestige. And while no longer Academia's absolute monarchs, Oxford and Cambridge are still the superpowers of English higher education.

We also go in for all kinds of measurements: the proportion of graduates of a particular liberal arts college who go on to acquire a doctorate; the number of books in a college library; the number of graduates of an American suburban high school who get accepted by the college of their first choice; the popularity of different universities among students. But we have barely begun to ask: What are the *results* in this school? What should they be?

These questions would have come up anyhow. In this century, education has become much too expensive not to be held accountable. As we saw earlier, expenditures on the school system in developed countries have skyrocketed from 2 percent of the GNP around 1913 to 10 percent eighty years later.

But schools are also becoming much too important not to be held accountable—for thinking through what their results should be, as well as for their performance in attaining these results. To be sure, different school systems will give different answers to these questions. But every school system and every school will soon be required to ask them, and to take them seriously. We will no longer accept the schoolteacher's age-old excuse for malperformance: "The students are lazy and stupid." With knowledge the central resource of society, lazy students or poor students are the responsibility of the school. There are then only schools that perform and schools that do not perform.

The schools are already losing their monopoly as providers of schooling. There has always been competition between different schools—in France with its intense rivalry between government and Catholic schools, or in the United States between different colleges and universities. In few industries is competition as keen or as ruthless as it is between "prestige schools" in developed countries. But increasingly the competition will be between schools and "non-schools," with different kinds of institutions entering the field, each offering a different approach to schooling.

> One example of what can be expected is the large American company, which is starting to compete with major business schools. It is marketing to other companies the executive-management program which it developed for its own managers, and is about to offer this program also to government agencies and the armed services. Another example is the Japanese *juku,* the "cram schools," which now enroll a very large proportion of Japanese middle and high school students. And there is the American publisher who recently launched a company to build six hundred schools within the next five years. They plan to charge moderate fees (no more than the average cost of a child in the public school), yet they are to be highly profitable. And they intend to promise results: "High test scores or your money back."

A good many of these ventures will surely fail. Still, they will be launched in large numbers.

As knowledge becomes the resource of post-capitalist society, the social position of school as "producer" and "distributive channel" of knowledge, and its monopoly, are both bound to be challenged. And some of the competitors are bound to succeed.

What will be taught and learned; how it will be taught and learned; who will make use of schooling; and the position of the school in society—all of this will change greatly during the ensuing decades. Indeed, no other institution faces challenges as radical as those that will transform the school.

But the greatest change—and the one we are least prepared for—is that the school will have to commit itself to results. It will have to establish its "bottom line," the performance for which it should be held responsible and for which it is being paid. *The school will finally become accountable.*

12

The Educated Person

POST-CAPITALIST SOCIETY deals with the environment in which human beings live and work and learn. It does not deal with the person. But in the knowledge society into which we are moving, individuals are central. Knowledge is not impersonal, like money. Knowledge does not reside in a book, a databank, a software program; they contain only information. Knowledge is always embodied in a person; carried by a person; created, augmented, or improved by a person; applied by a person; taught and passed on by a person; used or misused by a person. The shift to the knowledge society therefore puts the person in the center. In so doing it raises new challenges, new issues, new and quite unprecedented questions about the knowledge society's representative, the educated person.

In all earlier societies, the educated person was an ornament. He or she embodied *Kultur*—the German term which in its mixture of awe and derision is untranslatable into English (even "highbrow" does not come close). But in the knowledge society, the educated person is society's emblem; society's symbol; society's standardbearer. The educated person is the social "archetype"—to use the sociologist's term. He or she defines society's performance capacity. But he or she also embodies society's values, beliefs, commitments. If the feudal knight was the clearest embodiment of society in the early Middle Ages, and the "bourgeois" under Capitalism, the educated person will represent society in the post-capitalist society in which knowledge has become the central resource.

This must change the very meaning of "educated person." It must change the very meaning of what it means to be educated. It will thus predictably make the definition of an "educated person" a crucial issue. With knowledge becoming the key resource, the educated person faces new demands, new challenges, new responsibilities. *The educated person now matters.*

For the last ten or fifteen years a vigorous—often shrill—debate has been raging in American Academia over the educated person. Should there be one? Could there be one? And what should be considered "education" anyway?

A motley crew of post-Marxists, radical feminists, and other "antis" argues that there can be no such thing as an educated person—the position of those new nihilists, the "Deconstructionists." Others in this group assert that there can be only educated persons with each sex, each ethnic group, each race, each "minority" requiring its own separate culture and a separate—indeed, an isolationist—educated person. Since these people are mainly concerned with the "humanities," there are few echoes as yet of Hitler's "Aryan physics," Stalin's "Marxist genetics," or Mao's "Communist psychology." But the arguments of these anti-traditionalists recall those of the totalitarians. And their target is the same: the universalism that is at the very core of the concept of an educated person, whatever it may be called ("educated person" in the West, or *"bunjin"* in China and Japan).

The opposing camp—we might call them the "Humanists"—also scorns the present system. But it does so because it fails to produce a universally educated person. The Humanist critics demand a return to the nineteenth century, to the "liberal arts," the "classics," the German *Gebildete Mensch*. They do not, so far, repeat the assertion made by Robert Hutchins and Mortimer Adler fifty years ago at the University of Chicago that "knowledge" in its entirety consists of a hundred "great books." But they are in direct line of descent from the Hutchins-Adler "Return to Pre-Modernity."

Both sides, alas, are wrong. The knowledge society *must* have at its core the concept of the educated person. It will have to be a universal concept, precisely because the knowledge society is a society of knowledges and because it is global—in its money, its economics, its careers, its technology, its central issues, and above all, in its information. Post-capitalist society requires a unifying force. It requires a leadership group, which can focus local, particular, separate traditions onto a common and shared commitment to values, a common concept of excellence, and on mutual respect.

The post-capitalist society—the knowledge society—thus needs exactly the opposite of what Deconstructionists, radical feminists, or anti-Westerners propose. It needs the very thing they totally reject: a universally educated person.

Yet the knowledge society needs a different kind of educated person from the ideal for which the Humanists are fighting. They rightly stress the folly of their opponents' demand to repudiate the Great Tradition and the wisdom, beauty, knowledge that are the heritage of mankind. But a bridge to the past is not enough—and that is all the Humanists offer. The educated person needs to be able to bring his or her knowledge to bear on the present, not to mention molding the future. There is no provision for such ability in the proposals of the Humanists, indeed, no concern for it. But without it, the Great Tradition remains dusty antiquarianism.

In his 1943 novel *Das Glasperlenspiel* (*The Glass Bead Game*),* Hermann Hesse anticipated the sort of world the Humanists want—and its failure. The book depicts a brotherhood of intellectuals, artists, and Humanists who live a life of splendid isolation, dedicated to the Great Tradition, its wisdom and its beauty. But the

* Published in English as *Magister Ludi* (1949).

hero, the most accomplished Master of the Brotherhood, decides in the end to return to the polluted, vulgar, turbulent, strife-torn, money-grubbing reality—for his values are only fool's gold unless they have relevance to the world.

What Hesse foresaw more than fifty years ago is now in fact happening. "Liberal education" and "*Allgemeine Bildung*" are in crisis today because they have become a *Glasperlenspiel* which the brightest desert for crass, vulgar, money-grubbing reality. The ablest students appreciate the liberal arts. They enjoy them fully as much as did their great-grandparents, who graduated before World War I. For that earlier generation, liberal arts and *Allgemeine Bildung* remained meaningful throughout their lives, and defined their identity. They still remained meaningful for many members of my generation, which graduated before World War II—even though we immediately forgot our Latin and Greek. But all over the world today's students, a few years after they have graduated, complain that "what I have learned so eagerly has no meaning; it has no relevance to anything I am interested in or want to become." They still want a liberal arts curriculum for their own children—Princeton or Carleton; Oxbridge; Tokyo University; the *Lycée*; the *Gymnasium*—though mainly for social status and access to good jobs. But in their own lives they repudiate such values. They repudiate the educated person of the Humanists. Their liberal education, in other words, does not enable them to understand reality, let alone to master it.

Both sides in the present debate are largely irrelevant. Postcapitalist society needs the educated person even more than any earlier society did, and access to the great heritage of the past will have to be an essential element. But this heritage will embrace a good deal more than the civilization that is still mainly Western, the Judeo-Christian tradition, for which the Humanists are fighting. The educated person we need will have to be able to appreciate other cultures and traditions: the great heritage of Chinese, Japanese, Korean paintings and ceramics; the philosophers and religions of the Orient; and Islam, both as a religion and as a culture. The educated person also will have to be far less exclusively "bookish" than the product of the liberal education of the Humanists. He or she will need trained perception fully as much as analysis.

The Western tradition will, however, still have to be at the core, if only to enable the educated person to come to grips with the present, let alone the future. The future may be "post-Western"; it may be "anti-Western." It cannot be "non-Western." Its material civilization and its knowledges all rest on Western foundations: Western science; tools and technology; production; economics; Western-style finance and banking. None of these can work unless grounded in an understanding and acceptance of Western ideas and of the entire Western tradition.

> The early nineteenth-century West African who carved the wooden masks which the developed countries so eagerly collect knew nothing of the West and owed little to it. His descendant in West Africa who carves wooden masks today (and some are extraordinarily powerful) still lives in a mud hut in the tribal village. His country may not even be "underdeveloped" yet. Still, he has a radio, a TV set, and a motorbike. He uses new tools, all of them products of Western technology. He carves for an art dealer in Paris or New York. And his aesthetics owe as much to the German Expressionists and to Picasso as they do to his own West African ancestors.

The most profoundly "anti-Western" movement today is not Fundamentalist Islam. It is the revolt of the "Shining Path" in Peru—the desperate attempt of the descendants of the Incas to undo the Spanish Conquest, to go back to the Indians' ancient tongues of Quechua and Aymara, and to drive the hated Europeans and their culture back into the ocean. But this anti-Western rebellion finances itself by growing coca for the drug addicts of New York and Los Angeles. Its favorite weapon is not the Incas' slingshot; it is the car bomb.

Tomorrow's educated person will have to be prepared for life in a global world. It will be a "Westernized" world, but also increasingly a tribalized world. He or she must become a "citizen of the world"—in vision, horizon, information. But he or she will also have to draw nourishment from their local roots and, in turn, enrich and nourish their own local culture.

Post-capitalist society is both a knowledge society and a society of organizations, each dependent on the other and yet each very different in its concepts, views, and values. Most, if not all, educated persons will practice their knowledge as members of an organization. The educated person will therefore have to be prepared to live and work simultaneously in two cultures—that of the "intellectual," who focuses on words and ideas, and that of the "manager," who focuses on people and work.

Intellectuals see the organization as a tool; it enables them to practice their *technē*, their specialized knowledge. Managers see knowledge as a means to the end of organizational performances. Both are right. They are opposites; but they relate to each other as poles rather than as contradictions. They surely need each other: the research scientist needs the research manager just as much as the research manager needs the research scientist. If one overbalances the other, there is only non-performance and all-around frustration. The intellectual's world, unless counter-balanced by the manager, becomes one in which everybody "does his own thing" but nobody achieves anything. The manager's world, unless counterbalanced by the intellectual, becomes the stultifying bureaucracy of the "Organization Man." But if the two balance each other, there can be creativity and order, fulfillment and mission.

A good many people in the post-capitalist society will actually live and work in these two cultures at the same time. And many more should be exposed to working experience in both cultures, by rotation early in their careers—from a specialist's job to a managerial one, for instance, rotating the young computer technician into project manager and team leader, or by asking the young college professor to work part time for two years in university administration. And again, working as "unpaid staff" in an agency of the social sector will give the individual the perspective, the balance to respect both worlds, that of the intellectual and that of the manager.

All educated persons in the post-capitalist society will have to be prepared to *understand* both cultures.

For the educated person in the nineteenth century, *technēs* were not knowledge. They were already taught in the university and had become "disciplines." Their practitioners were "professionals," rather than "tradesmen" or "artisans." But they were not part of the liberal arts or the *Allgemeine Bildung*, and thus not part of knowledge.

University degrees in *technēs* go back a long way: in Europe, both the law degree and the medical degree as far as the thirteenth century. And on the Continent and in America—though not in England—the new engineering degree (first awarded in Napoleon's France a year or two before 1800) soon became socially accepted. Most people who were considered "educated" made their living practicing a *technē*—whether as lawyers, physicians, engineers, geologists, or increasingly in business (only in England was there esteem for the "gentleman" without occupation). But their job or their profession was seen as a "living," not a "life."

Outside their offices, the *technē* practitioners did not talk about their work or even about their disciplines. That was "shop talk"; the Germans sneered at it as *"Fachsimpeln."* It was even more derided in France: anyone who indulged in shop talk there was considered a boor and a bore, and promptly taken off the invitation lists of polite society.

But now that the *technēs* have become knowledges in the plural, they have to be integrated into knowledge. The *technēs* have to become part of what it means to be an educated person. The fact that the liberal arts curriculum they enjoyed so much in their college years refuses to attempt this is the reason why today's students repudiate it a few years later. They feel let down, even betrayed. They have good reason to feel that way. Liberal arts and *Allgemeine Bildung* which do not integrate the knowledges into a "universe of knowledge" are neither "liberal" nor *"Bildung."* They fall down on their first task: to create mutual understanding, that "universe of discourse" without which there can be no civilization. Instead of uniting, such disciplines only fragment.

We neither need nor will get "polymaths" who are at home in many knowledges; in fact, we will probably become even more specialized. But what we do need—and what will define the educated person in the knowledge society—is the ability to *understand* the various knowledges. What is each one about? What is it trying to do? What are its central concerns and theories? What major new insights has it produced? What are its important areas of ignorance, its problems, its challenges?

Without such understanding, the knowledges themselves will become sterile, will indeed cease to be "knowledges." They will become intellectually arrogant and unproductive. For the major new insights in every one of the specialized knowledges arise out of another, separate specialty, out of another one of the knowledges.

Both economics and meteorology are being transformed at present by the new mathematics of Chaos theory. Geology is being profoundly changed by the physics of matter, archaeology by the genetics of DNA typing, history by psychological, statistical, and technological analyses and techniques. An American, James M. Buchanan (b. 1919), received the 1986 Nobel Prize in Economics for applying recent economic theory to the political process and thereby standing on their heads the assumptions and theories on which political scientists had based their work for over a century.

The specialists have to take responsibility for making both themselves and their specialty understood. The media, whether magazines, movies, or television, have a crucial role to play. But they cannot do the job by themselves. Nor can any other kind of popularization. Specialties must be understood for what they are: serious, rigorous, demanding disciplines. This requires that the leaders in each of the knowledges, beginning with the leading scholars in each field, must take on the hard work of defining what it is they do.

There is no "Queen of the Knowledges" in the knowledge society. All knowledges are equally valuable; all knowledges, in

the words of the great medieval saint and philosopher St. Bona-
ventura, lead equally to the truth. But to make them paths to
truth, paths to knowledge, has to be the responsibility of the men
and women who own these knowledges. Collectively, they hold
knowledge in trust.

Capitalism had been dominant for over a century when Karl
Marx in the first volume of *Das Kapital* identified it (in 1867), as a
distinct social order. The term "Capitalism" was not coined until
thirty years later, well after Marx's death. It would therefore not
only be presumptuous in the extreme to attempt to write *The
Knowledge* today; it would be ludicrously premature. All that can
be attempted—all this book attempts—is to describe society and
polity as we begin the transition from the Age of Capitalism (also,
of course, the Age of Socialism).

But we can hope that a hundred years hence a book of this
kind, if not one entitled *The Knowledge*, can be written. That
would mean that we have successfully weathered the transition
upon which we have only just embarked. It would be as foolish to
predict the knowledge society as it would have been foolish to
predict in 1776—the year of the American Revolution, of Adam
Smith's *Wealth of Nations*, and of James Watt's steam engine—the
society of which Marx wrote a hundred years later. And it was as
foolish of Marx to predict in mid-Victorian Capitalism—and
with "Scientific infallibility"—the society in which we live now.

But one thing we can predict: the greatest change will be the
change in knowledge—in its form and content; in its meaning; in
its responsibility; and in what it means to be an educated person.

Acknowledgments

THIS BOOK OWES much to my long-time editor and friend Cass Canfield, Jr. He patiently endured countless proposals and outlines, and encouraged me at every step. He carefully read my manuscript and made most helpful suggestions and criticisms. Thanks are due also to another long-time friend, Marion Buhagiar, who read and reviewed the book's first completed draft and helped greatly in revising and editing it. And Ann Adelman, as often before, watched over sentence structure, syntax, and consistency with the keenest ear for language and its flow. The biographer of Frederick Winslow Taylor, Professor Ronald Greenwood of GMI, the General Motors Engineering and Management Institute in Flint, Michigan, critically read my comments on Taylor and Scientific Management (in Chapter 1). The last section of Chapter 6 owes a debt to the late Robert Greenleaf (especially to his wise little book, *Servant Leadership* [Paulist Press, 1977]), and to *Leadership as an Art*, by Max de Pree (Doubleday, 1990), as well as to a good many discussions with these two friends and with Dr. David Allan Hubbard, President of Fuller Theological Seminary in Pasadena, California.

My assistant Holly Hauck, over a long year, bravely coped with the vagaries of my handwriting. To all of them my warmest thanks.

Claremont, California
Thanksgiving Day, 1992

Index

Index

Index

Pareto, Vilfredo, 51
Pareto's Law, 131
Pascal, Blaise, 99
Patents, 28
Patriotism, 171–72
Pension funds, 6, 8, 67, 74–79, 80, 81, 82
Planning, 188–89
Plant community, 174
Plato, 26
Pluralist societies, 102–3
Poland, 177
Political integration, and the nation-state, 119–20
Political parties, 158
Political theory, and the nation-state, 10, 116
Politics
    and capital, 68–69
    and economic aid, 164
    and fiscal policy, 143
    and labor, 68–69
Populism, 124
Pork-Barrel State, 133–36, 164, 165
Post-capitalist polity, 4–6, 141–45, 156
Post-capitalist society
    as a developed world phenomena, 14–15
    divisions in the, 8–9
    emergence of the, 6–9, 11
    overview of, 4–6
    and post-capitalist polity, 4–6
    social challenge in the, 8
    structure of, 96
    as a transformation, 1
Post-capitalist society, and capitalist institutions, 7–8
Post-capitalist society, characteristics of, 4
Potter's wheel, 21
Power
    abuse of, 105
    and citizenship, 172
    and community, 173
    ethics of, 99
    and function, 105
    importance of, 104
    and knowledge, 47
    and the nation-state, 10–11
    and organizations, 97, 99, 102–6
    as an organizing force, 97
    and pluralist societies, 102–3
    and responsibility, 101, 102–6, 109
    social/political, 103–5
    and technology, 37
    and totalitarianism, 10
Prescott, William H., 116n
Printing press, 2

Process knowledge, 201–4
Production
    of information, 182
    of knowledge, 182, 185
    labor as a factor of, 68
    and manufacturing, 69–71
    and productivity, 85
Productivity
    and apprenticeships, 37
    of capital, 188
    and capitalists, 34, 36
    and class, 5, 20, 40, 95–96
    and command and control, 92
    and concentration, 90–92, 191
    and continuous education/learning, 92
    and costs, 38–39
    as dominant, 42–43
    and the economy, 188
    emergence of term, 37n
    and government, 94–95
    importance of, 193
    and income, 84, 131–32
    and intellectuals, 39
    of knowledge, 8, 20, 32–40, 45, 50, 186–88, 192–93
    and knowledge workers, 83–96
    and labor, 72
    and the long/short term, 191
    and management, 36, 190–92, 193
    and Marxism, 20, 32–33, 39
    and the megastate, 131–32
    and organizations, 83, 92, 93
    and outsourcing, 93–95
    prerequisites for, 91–92
    and production work, 85
    and the Productivity Revolution, 5, 20, 32–40, 42–43, 45
    and the proletariat, 38, 39
    and responsibility, 92, 109
    and service work, 169–70
    and service workers, 83–96, 168
    and the standard of living, 38
    and teams, 85–90
    and technology, 33
    and unions, 39
    and value, 8
    and what is known, 192–93
    and work, 33–36
Professional managers. See Managers
Profits, and costs, 81
Proletariat, 5, 22–23, 24, 31–32, 33, 38, 39, 64, 67
Protagoras, 26–27, 45–46
Protestant Reformation, 2
Protestantism, 2, 54
Public audit, 164–65
Purchasing power, 38